D0866368

THE EARLY PLAYS OF
JAMES A. HERNE
with ACT IV of "GRIFFITH DAVENPORT"

AMERICA'S LOST PLAYS

VOLUME VII

A series in twenty volumes of hitherto unpublished plays collected with the aid of the Rockefeller Foundation, under the auspices of the Dramatists' Guild of the Authors' League of America, edited with historical and bibliographical notes.

A complete list of volumes, with the names of plays contained in each, will be found on pages 162-3 of this volume.

PUBLISHED AND DISTRIBUTED BY
PRINCETON UNIVERSITY PRESS
PRINCETON, N.J.

The Early Plays of

James A. Herne

WITH ACT IV OF

GRIFFITH DAVENPORT

EDITED WITH AN INTRODUCTION BY

ARTHUR HOBSON QUINN

PRINCETON • NEW JERSEY

PRINCETON UNIVERSITY PRESS

• 1940 •

SET UP AND PRINTED
IN THE UNITED STATES OF AMERICA
BY PRINCETON UNIVERSITY PRESS
AT PRINCETON, NEW JERSEY

CONTENTS

INTRODUCTION

These plays of James A. Herne, now printed for the first time, represent him in the earlier stages of his career, with the exception of the fragment of *The Reverend Griffith Davenport.* He was born February 1, 1839, at Cohoes, N.Y., and made his stage début as George Shelby in *Uncle Tom's Cabin* at the Adelphi Theatre in Troy, in 1859. After playing several seasons with stock companies in Baltimore, Philadelphia and Washington, he became the leading man for Lucille Western, and his first visit to California, in 1868, was with her company. It was in the 'seventies, however, when he became the stage manager at Maguire's New Theatre in San Francisco, that he began to write plays. His great admiration for Dickens is reflected not only in some of these adaptations, which have perished, but also in his acting parts such as Caleb Plummer, Dan'l Peggotty and Captain Cuttle. Herne preferred to represent real life upon the stage, but he had also the actor's inherent love of romance and his first adaptation to survive in manuscript represents an interesting example of his collaboration with David Belasco, at all times a romantic artist.

Of even more importance for Herne's future career was his marriage with Katharine Corcoran, to whom he gave her first opportunity as an actress in 1877 and who, after their marriage in 1878, joined the Baldwin Theatre Stock Company. Her encouragement and her understanding of dramatic values were of inestimable advantage to Herne in his playwriting, and in his most important plays the leading part was interpreted by her with a skill which was amply recognized by contemporary dramatic criticism.

Within an Inch of His Life is a free adaptation of Emile Gaboriau's novel, *La Corde au Cou.* Miss Julie Herne is of the opinion that her father worked from an English translation, as his study of French began only in 1896. The relative shares of Herne and Belasco it is not possible now to assign accurately. Belasco's representation of the fire scene through red and yellow silk slips was one of his early successful bits of stage mechanics. The manuscript is not in the handwriting of either, but it remained in the possession of Herne and certain marginal notes are clearly in his script. The dramatization of *La Corde au Cou,* while it accentuated certain of the melodramatic elements of the original and even created new ones, is not on the whole unskilful. The painstaking details which French legal customs forced Gaboriau to insert, are done away with with a cheerful disregard of facts, amply justified by the directness of the play. While Herne and Belasco might have made a good scene out of the trial, the omission of the detective, Goudar, and his investigation of the illicit relations of Jacques de Boiscoran with the Comtesse de Claudieuse, as they are called in the novel, is a distinct improvement. The playwrights establish the relations of these two in Act I, Scene 2, which is not in the novel, but which is described much later by Jacques to his attorney. In the play the audience is put at once into possession of a knowledge of these relations, and suspicion is directed against the Comtesse. Her denunciation of Jacques is made the climax of the act. This greater emphasis makes Jacques' revelation of their relations more consistent with his rôle of hero. Another change was made by having Dionysia Chandore overhear the confession of Jacques to his counsel, and yet assert her love for him still. In the novel, she discovered his relation to the Comtesse by a slip of the attorney's tongue. The play thus carries over from the novel the strong motive of her devotion to her lover, but it establishes this motive earlier, and, in the hands of Katharine Corcoran, she was evidently an appealing figure on the stage.

In the novel, Jacques is condemned not to death but to twenty years' imprisonment, and his release is secured not only through Cocoleu's confession, but also through the Comte's dying statement that he believes Jacques innocent.

The most effective change came in the character of Cocoleu. In the novel he is simply an imbecile, devoted to his mistress, who reveals his crime to the detective under the influence of liquor. In the last scene of the play, however, his devotion is an active, not merely a passive force, and he comes of his own accord to the prison, and establishes much more convincingly the motive for the murder.

The Minute Men of 1774-1775 is the first surviving play of Herne's which may be considered entirely original. It represents a transitional stage in his development. The plot is conventional, and the historical background is not convincingly worked into the dramatic movement. Herne anticipated later writers, however, in making Lieutenant Smollet a natural, likable gentleman instead of the caricature which the British officer so often became in our drama of the Revolution. Ann Campbell may seem exaggerated for purposes of low comedy, but she was not unlike the pioneer type whose services to the Revolution are matters of record. The achievement of Herne in this play lay in the character of Dorothy Foxglove, written for Mrs. Herne. Whenever she appears, the stage takes on life. Instead of being merely receptive, like the usual romantic heroine, she is an active force, dominating the scene, but ruling it through her charm and spontaneity, which are reflected even in the manuscript. In the hands of Katharine Corcoran, they must have been irresistible.

The criticisms in the *Philadelphia Ledger* and the *Philadelphia Press* of April 7 speak of the effectiveness of the production, which was enthusiastically received by the audience.

Herne's next step in the progress toward realism is represented in *Drifting Apart*. The manuscript of this play has disappeared and the early form here printed under its first title, *Mary the Fishermen's Child,* underwent much revision before it saw the stage. It is hardly fair to judge Herne by this preliminary draft. The low-comedy scenes which he himself stigmatizes as "weak" are certainly overstressed.

What makes the play of especial interest, however, is the early use of the dream scene in Acts III and IV. Any competent dreamer will recognize the confusion of motivation in the third Act, especially in the relations of Mary and Percy, as quite in keeping with a dream in Jack's state of mind. Also quite natural, in a dream, was the transition to stark tragedy in the fourth Act. Such a scene as that which closed the fourth Act seems quite in keeping with modern stage technique. But in 1888 it was daring, for audiences still felt called upon to be shocked by such death scenes, unless they were placed in the past, and dignified by the glamour of poetry.

Drifting Apart, though it ran for two hundred and fifty performances, was not considered a financial success. According to Mrs. Herne, audiences disliked having their feelings harrowed by what turned out to be a dream. But the play attracted the attention of realists like William Dean Howells and Hamlin Garland, and Herne was encouraged to write his epoch making play, *Margaret Fleming*. *Shore Acres* followed and after a romantic play, *My Colleen,* which has been lost, came *The Reverend Griffith Davenport*. This was based upon a novel, *An Unofficial Patriot,* by Helen H. Gardener. Herne moulded this loosely constructed story into a unified drama to which contemporary criticism gave a high place for its sweep and color and for its character portrayal.

The unique manuscript of *Griffith Davenport* was burned in the fire which destroyed Herne Oaks. When the late Brander Matthews was in London in 1925, he was presented with the manuscript of the fourth Act, which is here printed. It had been found among the papers of the critic, William Archer, and his executors, knowing Archer's high opinion of Herne's work, felt it should be preserved in the United States. In a recent letter of C. Archer, he speaks of his late brother's attitude:

"In his [William Archer's] article on *The Development of American Drama* (*Harper's Monthly Magazine,* December 1920), speaking of the state of the drama in 1899, he says: 'In *Shore Acres* and *Sag Harbour* James A. Herne was producing delicately faithful pictures of rural life; while in *Griffith Davenport* (an unappreciated and now lost work) he had created an exquisitely true and beautiful drama of American history.' "

Brander Matthews loaned me the manuscript on his return and I had copies made for Mrs. Herne, for the collection of manuscripts in the Library of the University of Pennsylvania, and for Dr. Matthews. He stated to me at that time that it was his intention to deposit the original manuscript in the Brander Matthews Dramatic Museum at Columbia University. The manuscript has not been found, however, either at Columbia or among his papers. It would have again been lost if the copies had not been made. For the scenario of the other Acts, which is printed as an introduction to Act IV, I am indebted to Mrs. Herne and to Miss Julie Herne, who acted Emma West in the play.

I have deemed it best to print the plays, so far as possible, exactly as Herne wrote them. Students of the drama will be interested to have the stage directions reproduced just as a practical playwright of that era indicated them for his actors. Obvious mistakes in spelling and punctuation made by copyists have, however, been corrected.

It has not been possible to give complete casts of those who acted in the first productions of the plays. Information derived from T. Allston Brown's *History of the New York Stage,* from William Winter's *Life of Belasco,* from the newspapers and from Miss Julie Herne, has been incorporated in the casts as given. Unfortunately, no programs remain in Mrs. Herne's possession. The cast of *The Minute Men* was furnished by the courtesy of Mrs. Charles Wesley Phy, from the notes of her late husband, who at the time of his death had almost brought to completion his *History of the Philadelphia Stage from 1878 to 1890.*

WITHIN AN INCH OF HIS LIFE

CAST OF CHARACTERS

(*Grand Opera House, San Francisco, February 17, 1879*)

Jules de Dardeville	JAMES O'NEILL
Dr. Seignebos	J. W. JENNINGS
Count de Clairnot	JAMES A. HERNE
Cocoleau	LEWIS MORRISON
Galpin	A. D. BRADLEY
Seneschal	
Mechinet	
Folgat	
Magloire	
Blangin	
Ribot	WILLIAM SEYMOUR
Gaudry	JOHN N. LONG
Pierre	
Genevieve, *Countess de Clairnot*	ROSE WOOD
Dionysia Chandore	KATHARINE CORCORAN
Collette	
Gendarmes, Peasants, etc.	

ACT I.

SCENE 1: *Forest of Rochpommier. Time: Night. Enter Gaudry, a ragged poacher, R.1.E.*

GAU. A good night for poaching! Dark as pitch, and every keeper snug in bed! My traps are set and before morning will catch game enough to keep me a week. Hark! Some one comes. [*Looks off R.1.E.*] Who can it be? He who walks the forest of Rochpommier at this hour has business of more importance than gathering chestnuts. [*Enter Jules de Dardeville, hurriedly, R.1.E., with gun. See description in Act II.*]

JUL. A good path:—deserted, and not a soul stirring. So far, so good.

GAU. [*Aside, from concealment*] It is Jules de Dardeville, who is going to be married to the heiress, Miss Dionysia. I'd better be off! Poaching's dangerous business. [*Sneaks off L.1.E.*]

RIB. [*Outside R.1.E.*] Hello, there!

JUL. [*Starting*] Some one coming! It is too late to hide myself.

RIB. [*Entering R.1.E.*] Who's there?

JUL. A stranger; on his way to Brechy.

RIB. [*Aside, eyeing Jules closely*] On his way to Brechy? Well, he has taken a rather roundabout way to go to Brechy! [*Aloud*] Why, the high road would fetch you there in half the time.

JUL. [*Quickly*] I—I did not mean Brechy. I meant Seille.

RIB. Ha! Ha! Seille! Come, that's good! The nearest road to Seille is by the cross-road.

JUL. True! True!

RIB. True! Come, confess; confess at once! There's a woman in it. You're good-looking, like me! There's some one in the woods dying to see you; and you are dying to see some one. That's me! I don't deny it; I glory in it. Only I'm not so spooney as to get bothered and mixed up when I'm caught, eh? Ha! Ha! [*Laughing and poking Jules*]

JUL. [*Affecting a laugh*] Really, my friend, you mistake me! I am going to shoot tomorrow at Seille. You see! Here's my gun!

RIB. Yes. Ha! Ha! And so am I! Only it isn't exactly that kind of game. [*Bell strikes eleven*] Eleven o'clock! I must be off. I wish you luck anyhow; only, stranger, look out. It's dangerous business. [*Going L., aside*] That's

Jules de Dardeville. The sly dog don't know Ribot, but Ribot knows him. [*Exits chuckling*]

JUL. Dangerous business? Yes. Too true, too true! I have been observed, but not recognized. [*Examining gun*] One barrel empty. It's best to be prepared for an emergency. [*Takes cartridge box from pocket and puts cartridges in gun*] There! Thank Heaven tonight will decide this ugly affair and, I hope, forever. [*Exits L.1.E.*]

SCENE 2: *Valpinson by moonlight. Chateau with large massive doors. Balcony, steps, etc., C. Private entrance concealed by shrubbery, etc., etc. For full description of scene, see diagram.*[1] *Enter Countess Clairnot, hurriedly, from private entrance R.3.E. She looks around to see that she is not observed.*

COUNTESS. [*Coming C.*] Another hour and the dream of my life is broken. Yes, one short hour will end it all. Oh, Count Clairnot, you were cruel to forget that you were thirty years older than your wretched bride! I sacrificed myself to save my father's honor. But the restoration of that honor has been the ruin of a life! From that moment, I have hated and despised you! My father owes his life to you and your gold—and I—I, all my shame and despair. [*Turning towards R.3.E.*] He comes! Jules de Dardeville; the lover of Countess Clairnot. [*Laughs*] What would the world say, did they hear that? The world—[*Enter Jules R.3.E.*]

JUL. Genevieve.

COUNTESS. [*Coldly*] You have come. Jules de Dardeville, let us understand each other. You have proposed the mutual return of our correspondence. You say your mother wants you to marry. And you—what do you want?

JUL. I? [*Laughs*] I want nothing just now. But the thing will have to be done, sooner or later! A man must have a home—must have domestic relations, which the world acknowledges—

COUNTESS. And I—what am I to you?

JUL. You—you, Genevieve! I love you with all the strength of my heart! But we are separated by a gulf. You are married.

COUNTESS. Married. In other words, you have loved me as a toy. I have been the amusement of your idle hours;—that love, that romance, which every man must have. Now you are getting serious, and you leave me.

JUL. You—you have your home, your husband, your child—

COUNTESS. [*Bitterly*] Yes. I shall live here at Valpinson—when every place recalls to me your presence. I shall live here with my husband, whom I have betrayed; with my child, who is—[*Turning to him expressively*]

[1] No diagram was discovered with the manuscript.

JUL. Genevieve! This cannot last forever. Through my mother's earnest desire—not mine—I am betrothed to Dionysia Chandore. Shortly she will become my wife.

COUNTESS. [*Fiercely*] Your wife! No, Jules, no! That shall never be!

JUL. [*Quickly*] What would you do?

COUNTESS. Do? [*Slowly and deliberately*] I should give your letters to my husband.

JUL. You would not do that!

COUNTESS. [*Calmly*] Do not try me too far. [*Looking at him with a smile*] You are surprised at my determination, Jules de Dardeville. Hitherto, wives who have deceived their husbands have not held their lovers responsible. They have been betrayed but dared not cry aloud;—abandoned, only to submit and hide their tears—for who would pity them? But what no one dares, I dare! It shall not be said that in our common fault there are two parties, and that you shall have all the advantages and I must bear all the disgrace. What? You would be free, that you might console yourself with a new love! And I—I should have to sink under my shame and remorse. No! No! Such bonds as ours are not broken so easily. You belong to me! You are mine; and I shall defend you with such arms as I possess. I told you I valued my reputation more than my life—that my life was nothing. But now my reputation is less than my life. Go, marry Dionysia Chandore; and, as the priest joins your hands, my husband shall know all!

JUL. Madness!

COUNTESS. Aye, madness! Call it what you will. Call it love—to you a whim—a toy to be cast aside and trampled on—to me, life, death, desperation! Madness! Yes, madness that would sacrifice your life, your honor, with a smile on my lips, even though my heart should break.

JUL. Genevieve, we *must* part—it is for the best.

COUNTESS. Part! I inspire you with horror, do I? You would be free? Free! Beware! Beware!

JUL. Not so loud!—

COUNTESS. What do I care? What does it matter? Happiness awaits you, a new life, full of intoxicating hope. It is quite natural that *you* should dread discovery. *I,* whose life is ended, and who have nothing to look for—I, in whom you have killed every hope—I am not afraid.

JUL. [*Aside*] She is determined. But Jules de Dardeville never was afraid of an enemy; not even the Count Clairnot! [*Clutching his gun. Aloud*] You say you love me?

COUNTESS. Madly! Passionately!

JUL. Then in the name of that love, I appeal to you to release me.

COUNTESS. To wed another? Never! Never!

JUL. If I had foreseen this, our acquaintance never would have existed.

COUNTESS. Acquaintance? You confess then that you have never loved me!

JUL. You know the contrary.

COUNTESS. Still you think of abandoning me for another—for this Dionysia.

JUL. You are married. You cannot be mine!

COUNTESS. [*Quickly*] Then if I were free—

JUL. Free? You would be my wife.

COUNTESS. [*Aside, taking stage*] His wife! If I were free, I would be his wife! God! Luckily that thought never occurred to me before. Murder!

JUL. Calm yourself, Genevieve. This marriage which I mentioned is not my doing but that of my family. I have had no hand in it. My father called on M. de Chandore and asked him for the hand of his daughter. I have been publicly acknowledged as her betrothed and they themselves have fixed the wedding day.

COUNTESS. Is this true?

JUL. I swear it!

COUNTESS. You are not deceiving me, Jules?

JUL. Deceiving you? Why should I? I have loved you always—I love you still.

COUNTESS. But she—Dionysia—loves you. That love which is my disgrace is her honor.

JUL. But my love is, and always shall be, yours.

COUNTESS. [*With joy*] Oh, Jules! [*Recovering herself*] I believe you! I must believe you!

JUL. [*Aside*] At any price, I must have those letters.

COUNTESS. Jules, promise me one thing—till I of my own free will release you, you will never, never marry this Dionysia Chandore.

JUL. I promise! Where is the Count Clairnot?

COUNTESS. Confined to his room. He thinks I am sitting up with my child. But now to the business that brings you here. You think it best that we destroy our letters?

JUL. Yes. We cannot foresee events. The Count may discover them.

COUNTESS. True! Where are mine?

JUL. Here they are. [*Takes packet from pocket*]

COUNTESS. And here are yours. [*Produces them*]

JUL. [*Quickly*] We'll burn them!

COUNTESS. [*Gives them to him*] You see, Jules, I trust you. [*Jules goes to shrubbery R. lights both packets and then throws them out of sight*]

COUNTESS. [*As he comes down*] And that is all—all that remains of five years of our life, of our love, and of our vows—ashes!

JUL. Genevieve, forgive me all this bitterness. I, too, am unhappy—unhappy as yourself. But remember we are separated by an impassable gulf—society, family, marriage. In a word, the world stands between our loves. My family decides I must marry. Prudence compels it. I must go my way, and you yours. But till you of your own free will release me and break the chains that bind us I will remain faithful to my promise. Calm yourself. Do not grieve me more. Genevieve, promise me.

COUNTESS. [*Turns from him*] Spare me! I promise nothing! Go! Go! [*Crosses L.*]

JUL. Good-bye! Let us part friends. [*Offers his hand*]

COUNTESS. [*Taking it*] Good-bye.

JUL. [*Going R. turns and looks at Countess for a moment. She stands as immovable as a statue*] Genevieve! Farewell! [*Exits quickly through private entrance R.3. A slight pause. The Countess then suddenly realizes that she is alone*]

COUNTESS. [*With a cry*] His wife! [*Rising*] If I were free, I would be his wife. What terrible thought is darkly hidden in those words! [*In a hoarse whisper*] Murder! Murder! [*Exits greatly agitated R.3.E. A fire starts up from the place where Jules fired the letters and reaches to the house; and spreads till the whole building is in flames. Slight hurry inside. Cries of "fire" heard within. Count Clairnot rushes from doors C. and stands on steps*]

COUNT. Fire! Fire! Help! Help! [*At the same moment a shot is fired from shrubbery of private entrance.* NOTE: *The gun-barrel must be pushed forward enough to let the audience see the discharge, but not who discharges it. The Count staggers forward*]

COUNT. I am murdered! Assassin! [*He staggers towards shrubbery. Just before he reaches it, another shot is fired from the same place. The Count reels and falls C.*] Help! Murder! Help! [*Hurry within. Loud cries of "fire," general commotion and conflagration. Servants enter from house, and peasantry, citizens, etc., from all directions*]

PIERRE. [*Seeing Count*] What! The Count murdered!

OMNES. Murdered? [*Enter Countess from R.3.E.*]

COUNTESS. My husband! Murdered! The house in flames! [*The screams of a child heard in house*]

COUNTESS. My God! My child! Save her!

OMNES. It is impossible!

COUNTESS. [*Sinking on her knees*] Oh, wretched, wretched Genevieve! My child! She is lost! [*Suddenly the C. doors which are enveloped in flames are burst open and the idiot, Cocoleau, appears half blinded with smoke and fire carrying the child of the Countess*]

COCO. [*Coming down*] No! No! Ha! Ha! Ha! Saved, saved! [*Laughs idiotically. House falls with a crash*]

ACT II.

SCENE: *Chamber in the house of M. Seneschal, the mayor of Valpinson. Time: Night. Large C. doors. Doors R. and L.2.E. Count Clairnot on sofa R.H. Doctor Seignebos standing near table, arranging bandages, etc. Countess at foot of sofa kneeling. Mechinet standing at table with writing materials down L. Galpin at rear C. Two Gendarmes at C. doors. Gendarmes at door R. and L.*

COUNT. [*With effort*] My friends, you see the year 1871 is a fatal year. It has left me nothing but a handful of ashes.

SEN. Thank Heaven, you are safe.

COUNT. Who knows? I am suffering terribly!

COUNTESS. Courage, husband, courage!

COUNT. Pardon me, dear Genevieve, pardon me, if I show any want of fortitude.

DR. S. [*Addressing Omnes*] You see, gentlemen, he's in a bad plight! Wounds of this kind, although apparently not of a serious nature at first, often prove fatal.

GAL. [*Coming forward, to Doctor*] Therefore, Doctor, I am here. A crime has been committed. The criminal must be tracked, discovered, convicted, and punished! [*With great authority*] Therefore, I request your assistance and the assistance of those around me, in the name of the *Law!* [*Turning to Doctor*] Have you any objection to my questioning your patient?

DR. S. It would certainly be better for him to be left alone. I have made him suffer quite enough already. But if it must be—

GAL. It must be.

DR. S. Well, then, make haste.

GAL. [*Takes seat, beside the Count, at sofa*] Are you strong enough to answer my questions?

COUNT. Yes, yes, quite.

GAL. Then tell me all you know of the events of last night.

COUNT. I know but little. Shortly after the bell had struck eleven, a bright blaze flashed upon my window. Amazed, yet half-asleep, I was quickly aroused by the crash of something falling and the cry of "Fire." I rushed down stairs, but had hardly made a step, when I felt a fierce pain in my right side and heard a shot. I remembered I had that very evening left my gun in the shrubbery on the right of the steps. I endeavored, as best I could, to reach it and defend myself from the assassin, when directly from the shrubbery the assassin fired again, and after that all is blank.

GAL. [*Interestedly*] You did not see the assassin then?

COUNT. [*Shakes his head*] No.

GAL. Who can tell us what happened after you fell?

COUNT. Probably my wife, the Countess.

GAL. True! The Countess, no doubt, got up when you rose.

COUNT. My wife had not gone to bed. [*Galpin turns quickly to Countess, who avoids his glance*] Bertha, our little child, has been very ill. My wife was sitting up with her.

GAL. [*Suspiciously*] Exactly. [*To Countess*] When, and how did *you* become aware of the situation?

COUNTESS. My husband has told you I was sitting up with little Bertha. I was tired, for I had not gone to bed the night before, and had fallen into a doze when a sudden noise and light aroused me. Just then I heard a shot, quickly followed by another, and then cries for help! I hurried down in great haste. The front door was open and by the light of the flames I beheld my husband lying on the ground! Remembering my child, I beseeched the people to save it, but none would dare to venture, for the flames had enveloped everything. Then Cocoleau rushed from amidst the burning mass, bearing my child from the very jaws of death!

COUNT. Brave fellow!

GAL. Cocoleau—and who is Cocoleau?

DR. S. An idiot! An imbecile!

COUNTESS. This fire will probably ruin us! But what matters that so long as my husband and my child are safe!

DR. S. [*Rising*] Now sir, I hope you'll let me have my patient again.

GAL. Sir, I appreciate your duties, but mine are no less important.

DR. S. [*Sitting down*] Fudge!

GAL. Consequently, you will be pleased, sir, to grant me five minutes more.

DR. S. Ten, if it must be, sir. Only, I warn you that every minute henceforth may endanger the life of my patient.

GAL. I have only one more question to ask. [*To Count*] Where were you standing, and where do you think the murderer was standing, at the moment when the crime was committed?

COUNT. I was standing, as I told you, on the threshold of my door facing the courtyard. The murderer must have been standing some twenty yards off, on my right, behind a pile of wood.

GAL. [*Turning to Doctor*] You heard what he said, sir. It is for you now to aid justice by telling us at what distance the murderer must have been when he fired.

DR. S. I don't pretend to solve riddles.

GAL. Oh, have a care, sir! Justice, whom I here represent, has the right and the means to enforce respect. You are a physician, sir, and your medical science enables you to answer this question with almost mathematical accuracy.

DR. S. [*Aside*] Mathematical fiddlesticks!

GAL. What distance was the assassin from the Count when he fired?

DR. S. A conundrum! I give it up!

GAL. Have a care, sir! I can enforce the law.

DR. S. Then to answer you plainly, sir, it all depends upon the species of weapon used; whether it be a cannon, a gun, or a pistol. [*Sitting down*]

GAL. [*Enraged*] Remember, sir, that—

OMNES. [*Outside*] Death to the incendiary! Death to the assassin! [*Enter Pierre C. L.*]

PIERRE. [*Hurriedly*] A citizen and one of the firemen have been missing since the fall of the north wall. We have just discovered their remains among the ruins.

COUNT. Great Heavens! And I was complaining of my losses! Two men killed! Murdered! Poor men! Their bravery has cost them dear!

OMNES. [*Outside*] Death to the incendiary! Death to the assassin!

GAL. [*To Gendarmes at C. D.*] Admit the people. [*Gendarmes open doors C. Enter Peasants*]

OMNES. Death to the incendiary! Death to the assassin!

GAL. [*To Peasants*] You are right, good people! But we must first discover the criminal. Some one among you probably knows something. [*Pierre exits quickly C. Noise off C. Enter Pierre and a Peasant pushing Cocoleau in front of them. Cocoleau slightly resists*]

PIERRE. [*Pushing Cocoleau forward*] He knows something!

PEASANTS. Make him tell! Make him tell! [*Cocoleau stares around half-frightened, then suddenly starts to go off door C. Pierre, with Peasants, stops Cocoleau and pushes him down C. again*]

GAL. [*To Pierre*] Who is this, my good fellow?

PIERRE. Cocoleau.

GAL. Oh! So this is Cocoleau?

PIERRE. He knows something. He said so himself.

PEASANTS. Make him tell! Make him tell!

GAL. Aha! That is what we want. [*To Cocoleau*] Cocoleau?

COCO. [*Glances from one person to another idiotically, then looks at Galpin*] Eh?

DR. S. Stay, sir. You don't really mean to examine this fellow as a witness?

GAL. And why not?

DR. S. Because he cannot possibly understand your questions. He's a fool! An ass! And an ass is a fool; and a fool is a natural born ass!

GAL. [*Decidedly*] I know *my* duty, sir!

DR. S. [*Pompously*] And I know *my* duty, sir! Consider, sir, if this fellow should make a formal charge against any one! [*Cocoleau looks frightened at Dr. Seignebos*]

COUNT. At all events it was he who saved our child. Come nearer, Cocoleau. [*Cocoleau first hesitates, then finally steps nearer Count*] Come nearer. No one here would harm you. See, here is the Countess. She has been very kind to you.

COCO. [*Looks at Countess tenderly*] Good—dear—dear—lady!

GAL. Madam, request him to speak. He knows something. [*Countess starts*]

GAL. He seems attached to you and perhaps, if you will ask him, will tell us—

COUNTESS. [*Recovering herself*] Cocoleau, do not be afraid. Tell us what you know.

COCO. [*Reassured, stutters*] I—am—not—afraid.

DR. S. [*Rising*] Once more, I protest!

GAL. [*To Dr. Seignebos*] Sit down, sir!

DR. S. Fudge! [*Takes seat*]

COUNT. [*To Galpin*] It may be dangerous to question an irresponsible party.

GAL. [*Decidedly*] Gentlemen, I must beg to proceed in my own way. You will be silent. [*To Cocoleau*] Cocoleau, my boy, listen, and try to understand what I am going to say. [*Cocoleau nods head and looks stupidly*]

GAL. There has been a fire—

COCO. [*Knowingly*] Fire!

GAL. Yes, fire—which has burned down the house of your benefactor—fire which has killed two good men.

COCO. [*Repeats*] Killed—two—men.

GAL. But that is not all! They have tried to murder! Do you see him there in his bed, wounded and covered with blood? [*Cocoleau turns his face slowly to Count*]

GAL. Do you see the Countess, how she suffers?

COCO. [*Turning and looking at Countess with a look of pity and love*] Yes.

GAL. All these misfortunes are the work of a wicked man, a vile assassin! You hate him, don't you? You hate him?

COCO. [*Savagely, through his teeth*] Ye—yes!

GAL. You want him to be punished?

COCO. Yes! Yes!

GAL. Well then, you must help us to find him out so that the Gendarmes may catch him and put him in jail. [*Cocoleau hangs down his head, then glances from under his shaggy hair and looks furtively around the room, finally resting his eyes on the Countess*]

GAL. Do you hear me, my good boy?

COCO. Ye—yes!

GAL. And you will speak? [*Cocoleau slowly eyeing Countess, nods his head*]

GAL. [*With satisfaction*] Good! Then where did you spend last night?

COCO. [*Repeats the question, then answers*] In—the—courtyard.

GAL. Were you asleep when the fire broke out?

COCO. [*Quickly*] No!

GAL. Did you see it commence?

COCO. [*Long pause. He thinks, then answers suddenly*] Yes!

GAL. How did it commence? [*Cocoleau shakes his head; won't answer. Looks towards Countess with the timid expression of a dog who tries to read something in his master's eyes*]

COUNTESS. Yes, Cocoleau, tell us how it commenced.

COCO. [*With a flash of intelligence*] They—they set it afire!

GAL. On purpose?

COCO. Yes!

GAL. Who?

COCO. A—gentleman.

DR. S. [*Rising*] I protest! Such an examination is sheer folly!

GAL. [*Loudly to Dr. Seignebos*] Sit down, sir!

DR. S. [*Sitting*] Fudge!

GAL. Did you see the gentleman?

COCO. Yes!

GAL. Do you know who he is?

COCO. Very—very—well!

GAL. What is his name? [*General interest manifested*]

COCO. [*Slight pause*] Jules—Jules—de—de—Dardeville!

COUNT. Absurd!

DR. S. [*Keeping seat, triumphantly*] There! I told you so!

SENE. [*To Galpin*] If I were you, I'd attach no importance to the answer and consider it not given.

GAL. No. I shall proceed.

DR. S. [*Rising*] Proceed to what, sir? To array this idiot against your friend, Jules de Dardeville? Why the thing is ridiculous! You know that such a crime in him is actually impossible! And yet, without any evidence except the ravings of this idiot, you would publicly disgrace the man whom you pretend to be your friend, and whom you have dined with a hundred times, and who is universally respected by us all!

GAL. [*Sternly*] Nevertheless, gentlemen, I know my duty and shall proceed. [*To Cocoleau*] Do you know, my boy, what you say? Do you know that you are accusing a man of a horrible crime?

COCO. I—I—am—telling the—truth.

GAL. Jules de Dardeville set Valpinson on fire?

COCO. [*With conviction*] Yes.

GAL. How did he do it? [*Cocoleau pauses*]

GAL. Speak!

COCO. [*With countless contortions and painful efforts to speak commences*] I saw Jules de Dardeville—pull out—some—papers from his—pocket—light them—put them in—in shrubbery—near château!

COUNTESS. [*Aside, with a cry*] Oh!

[NOTE: *The actor playing the part of Cocoleau should study the business of Jules in Act I and go through same business here*]

GAL. [*To Cocoleau*] Now, good Cocoleau, since you have told us that Jules de Dardeville set the château on fire, tell us who fired upon the Count.

COCO. Who fired? [*Looks around, eyes the Countess, smiles with assurance*] Why—Jules de Dardeville—after—he—set—the—house—on—fire. Master—came—out—at—the—door—and—he—fired—from—the—trees. Master—fell! [*Laughs idiotically*] Ha! Ha! I saw it all! I saw it all! Yes! Ha! Ha!

GAL. If you saw it all, why didn't you seize the assassin?

COCO. [*Shakes his head*] Ha! Ha! Might get shot myself! Yes! Ha! Ha! Might get shot myself!

GAL. Since you saw it was Jules de Dardeville, tell us how he was dressed.

COCO. [*Looks at his own clothes, laughs*] Straw hat—short jacket—boots up here—[*Motioning*]—and gun.

DR. S. This is monstrous! To listen to the ravings of an idiot!

COUNT. Yes, I think myself, it's somewhat ridiculous to allow an honest man to be arraigned by this Cocoleau, who can scarcely remember from one hour to the other. Jules de Dardeville and myself had once a landsuit that culminated in a deadly quarrel. Still he is an honorable man and, although we once came near exchanging shots, I would as soon vouch for his honor as my own.

GAL. [*To Cocoleau*] Enough. [*Motions Cocoleau away. Cocoleau draws back and laughs meaninglessly, looking at Countess*]

DR. S. [*To Galpin*] What are you going to do?

GAL. I am going to prosecute. [*Noise outside center*] What is that? [*Enter Ribot and Gaudry C.*]

RIB. [*To Galpin, enquiringly*] The magistrate?

GAL. Yes. Can you throw any light upon this affair?

RIB. Yes. There was something suspicious happened to me last night.

GAL. [*To Mechinet*] Mechinet, here is another statement. [*To Ribot*] Well, sir, proceed.

RIB. Last night I was going through the forest of Rochpommier and, as I came near Valpinson, just as the bell struck eleven, I met a man hurrying along and acting as though he didn't want anyone to know much about him. He said he was going to Brechy, but when I told him he wasn't on the Brechy road, he looked confused and said he meant Seille. And I knew he lied, for if he was going to Seille he'd have taken the cross-roads—

GAL. Did you notice his dress?

RIB. Yes. He wore a straw hat, hunting jacket, and over-boots. He had a gun in his hand.

GAL. [*Interestedly*] Indeed! Could you swear to this?

RIB. Yes.

GAL. Did you recognize him as anyone you had seen before?

RIB. Yes—Jules de Dardeville. [*General movement*]

GAL. Jules de Dardeville! [*With satisfaction, to Mechinet*] Mechinet, have you taken down this witness's statement carefully?

MECH. Yes.

GAL. [*To Ribot*] That will do. [*Ribot bows and draws back*]

GAL. Now then, the next witness. [*Gaudry comes down*] Now then, my man, tell us what *you* know.

GAU. Last night I was in the forest of Rochpommier—

GAL. [*Interrupting*] Ah! You rascal! What were you doing there?

GAU. That's where I sleep, sir, on the leaves among the brushwood, for the sake of the fresh air.

GAL. Why do you sleep there?

GAU. So as to get up in the morning early. I pick chestnuts, sir, for the market.

GAL. Yes, I see. Go on.

GAU. Well, sir, I heard a noise, sir, and looking around, I saw a man coming along with a gun, talking to himself excited like, and going towards Valpinson. Shortly afterwards, I sees a blaze there and who should come back but the same man, going on just as before, only hurrying more and never looking back, but walking faster than a man could run.

GAL. You recognized him both times?

GAU. Yes.

GAL. Are you sure?

GAU. I would stake my life.

GAL. Then state in the presence of all, his name.

GAU. Jules de Dardeville.

GAL. Enough. Is there anyone else who knows anything. [*Pause*] None. Then we shall close the examination. You see, gentlemen, I was right. What, at first, was merely a doubt, gathered into a suspicion and then, at last facts. Cold, stern facts, promising actual proof, point in the direction of Jules de Dardeville! [*Noise off C. Enter Jacques*][1]

JAC. We have just discovered something, sir. [*Showing cartridge to Galpin*]

GAL. [*Taking cartridge from Jacques*] Why it is a cartridge! Where did you find this?

JAC. We found it near the shrubbery where the assassin concealed himself. He, no doubt, dropped it there last night.

COUNT. [*To Galpin*] Let me see it. [*Galpin gives cartridge to Count*] I can tell, at least, if the weapon used against me was my own, or that of another. [*Examines it*] No such cartridge as this belonged to me. [*Hands cartridge to Galpin*]

SENE. That cartridge was evidently the property of the assassin. He dropped it providentially as an evidence of his guilt. The weapon Jules de Dardeville used was the Remington and the only one of that make in the district. Examine the cartridge. If it is not a Remington it proves his innocence.

[1] There is no character given in the cast as "Jacques."

GAL. [*Examines cartridge. Starts triumphantly. To Seneschal*] There! Read for yourself! [*Hands cartridge to Seneschal*]

SENE. [*Examines cartridge. Starts*] Heavens! It is so! He is guilty!

DR. S. Guilty? Impossible! What would be his motive for such a crime? M. Jules de Dardeville has nothing to lose. Do you know among all your friends a happier man than he is? Young, handsome, rich, esteemed! Besides there is another fact which will at once remove all suspicion. M. Jules de Dardeville is desperately in love with the beautiful Dionysia Chandore.

COUNTESS. [*Aside, starting*] In love with Dionysia Chandore?

DR. S. And she returns his love. [*Countess clutches her hands*]

DR. S. And tomorrow is the day fixed for his marriage. He told me so himself last night.

COUNTESS. [*Aside, unable to control herself*] Wretch! He has lied to me!

DR. S. Gentlemen, I tell you it is impossible!

COUNTESS. [*Rising quickly, full of hate and anger*] Impossible? And why impossible? Did he not hate my husband? Has he not in a quarrel threatened his life? Does not a chain of indisputable evidence wind itself, link by link, around him? You think it nothing if he had robbed me of my husband, yet you melt at the thoughts of tearing him from his *beautiful Dionysia Chandore!* Yes, I believe him guilty! May Heaven bring down on his head the misery he has inflicted on mine!

GAL.[2] Calm yourself, madam! Calm yourself! Justice shall be done!

ACT III.

SCENE: *The prison at Sauveterre, overlooking courtyard. Large grated window C. with balcony exterior. Door L.3.E. with steps to stage. Balcony runs from door to window, exterior C. Jules seated at table L.H. Noise of unlocking door.* [*Enter Blangin*]

BLAN. Prisoner!

JUL. [*Raising his head*] Well?

BLAN. The magistrate. [*Admits Galpin, Seneschal and Mechinet*]

JUL. [*Approaching and offering his hand to Seneschal*] Ah! My old friend! [*Seneschal takes Jules' hand and shakes it heartily*] And you, too, Galpin! [*Offering his hand*]

GAL. [*Sternly refusing hand*] Wait, sir.

JUL. What? You do not know me? I do not understand all this! Probably you can explain. As for myself, I know nothing! Not even the cause

[2] This speech is crossed out in the manuscript and was evidently not used in the acting version.

of my arrest—thanks to the gendarmes who brought me so quietly here. Not a word could I get from them, only that I should know all soon enough. Perhaps you have come to enlighten me?

GAL. I have. Jules de Dardeville, a terrible charge has been brought against you! Unfortunately, I am a magistrate, sir. It is on your answers to my questions that your honor, your liberty, perhaps your very life, depend.

JUL. [*Surprised*] My life?

GAL. Yes, sir—your life. First, you are charged with setting fire to the Château of Valpinson.

JUL. What! I? Come, come, Galpin! You know me better than that!

SENE. [*Aside, to Galpin*] That man is certainly innocent. [*Aloud*] But not only are you charged with setting fire to the château, but also with murder!

JUL. [*Intensely surprised*] Murder?

GAL. Yes, murder.

JUL. And you, my old friend, Galpin, are my prosecutor? Impossible!

GAL. We shall have to forget our relations, sir. It is not as a friend I have come to see you, but as a magistrate.

JUL. If anyone, in my presence, had dared to accuse you of a crime, I should have defended you till absolutely undeniable evidence had proved your guilt, and even then I should have pitied you. But *you!* I am accused falsely, wrongfully—and you, my friend, not only believe the charge, but hasten to become my judge! Well, Galpin, I know you now.

GAL. [*Motions Mechinet to table*] Enough, sir! You forget our present positions.

JUL. I shall forget them no longer. Proceed. I am at your service. [*Mechinet goes to table L., takes seat, places writing materials on table, and proceeds to take down the examination*]

GAL. You were out last night?

JUL. Yes.

GAL. You took your gun—a Remington?

JUL. I did.

GAL. The only Remington in this district?

JUL. I believe so. I ordered it directly from the maker.

GAL. So you must have been on the spot where such a cartridge as this was found?

JUL. [*Takes cartridge and examines it*] Not of necessity. [*Aside*] Heavens! It is mine! How did it come there? Ah! I must have dropped it in taking the letters from my pocket. [*Handing back the cartridge*] Yes, it is a Remington. I cannot explain it.

GAL. You cannot? Now then, I beg you will give us an account of how you spent last night, between eight and eleven o'clock. [*Pause. Jules becomes greatly agitated, but quickly recovers himself*] Consider! Take your time and answer frankly, for remember, your life depends upon the question.

JUL. How do I know? I walked about.

GAL. That is no answer. You went through the forest of Rochpommier?

JUL. No, I did not.

GAL. Jules de Dardeville, you are not telling the truth.

JUL. Sir!

GAL. Do not attempt to deny it. Two witnesses will swear to what I say.

JUL. Two witnesses?

GAL. Yes. You told one of them you were going to Brechy, then corrected yourself and said to Seille. Jules de Dardeville, you went neither to Brechy or to Seille. You went to Valpinson. Last night, between eleven and twelve, Valpinson was burned to the ground!

JUL. Ah!

GAL. A private individual and a fireman perished in the flames; the Count Clairnot was shot by an assassin; and strong reasons point to you, Jules de Dardeville, as the incendiary and murderer!

JUL. Horrible!

GAL. You are charged with these crimes. It is for you to exculpate yourself.

JUL. [*In despair*] How can I? How can I?

GAL. Humph! If you are innocent, nothing is easier. Tell us where you were between eight and twelve o'clock last night.

JUL. [*Firmly*] I've told you all I can.

GAL. Then I must commit you for trial.

JUL. As you please.

GAL. Then you confess?

JUL. What?

GAL. That you are guilty?

JUL. No! I am innocent!

GAL. Prove it.

JUL. [*Turning away*] I can prove nothing.

GAL. [*Aside*] The greatest criminal case in the calendar! I'm sure of promotion! My fortune's made! On the other hand, if I should fail, his powerful and wealthy friends would ruin me. But nothing can save him! He will have to go to the guillotine, or to the galleys. [*Goes up*]

JUL. [*To Galpin*] A word before you go. Do you believe me guilty?

GAL. [*Coldly*] That is not for me to say. You have refused to answer my questions. I am but the representative of the law. [*Exits through door*]

JUL. And you, good Seneschal? [*Taking his hand*]

SENE. No! Never! Courage! Courage, my boy! In spite of appearances, I am still your friend. [*Exit Mechinet and Seneschal through door*]

JUL. [*Sinking into seat at table*] There is one, at least, who believes me innocent. [*Enter Blangin*]

BLAN. Prisoner, a lady to see you.

JUL. A lady? Who? [*Enter Dionysia*] Dionysia!

DION. Jules! [*They embrace. Exit Blangin and locks door*]

JUL. You here! You here? You have come to see Jules de Dardeville, even in a felon's cell?

DION. Why should I hesitate? Your honor is at stake, and your honor is my honor, as your life is my life!

JUL. And do you look upon me as the guilty wretch that some would deem me?

DION. No, Jules! By the sacred memory of my mother, I assure you that I have never doubted your innocence, even for a moment!

JUL. [*Embraces her*] Dear, dear Dionysia!

DION. They say that you will only have to prove that you were elsewhere at the time and all will be well.

JUL. Alas, I cannot!

DION. You cannot?

JUL. No, Dionysia, it is impossible!

DION. Ah, Jules, I am sure you could if you would. You are not aware of the danger you run, you do not know—

JUL. Yes, Dionysia, I know! I know that the guillotine or the galleys are at the end, and yet I must keep silent.

DION. You have not considered—

JUL. Considered? What do you think I have been doing all these dreadful hours since my arrest?

DION. Then why do you not speak? I, your Dionysia, your betrothed, beseech you—Jules de Dardeville, speak!

JUL. I dare not!

DION. Why not?

JUL. Because it would not establish my innocence if I did.

DION. My God! What do you say?

JUL. I say that there are circumstances which upset our reason—unheard of circumstances—which makes one even doubt one's very self. Everything accuses me, everything overwhelms me! I am neither a child, nor a coward, but I have measured the danger and I know it is fearful!

DION. And cannot you even confide it to me—your betrothed—your Dionysia?

JUL. To you less than to anyone else! Your mind is too pure. I would not have it stained by the slime into which fate has thrown me! [*Steps back from her. Then with uplifted hands*] Oh, Dionysia, leave me! Leave me! You do not know me!

DION. [*Springing towards him, terrified*] I do not know you? What do you mean?

JUL. Nothing! Nothing! Do not ask me!

DION. Why? Have I not the right? Am I not your betrothed? Have you not said you loved me, and have I not accepted your love?

JUL. Yes—yes!

DION. And when I have thus willingly placed my life in your care, have I not proved my trust?

JUL. You have—you have!

DION. Then why can you not place an equal confidence in me?

JUL. Oh, Dionysia!

DION. Why, standing here today, innocent, yet charged with crime, do you not dare speak? Not even to me? Do you think I am a child, from whom the truth must be concealed? Am I in your eyes of such a trivial nature as not to comprehend the importance of a secret that seals your lips and holds your life in jeopardy? Jules, Jules, you have no faith in me! You do not really love me! [*Sinking at his feet*]

JUL. [*Raising her*] If you knew what seals my lips, it would make you wretched! I have given you pain enough! I would not make your young life more unhappy! Were I to speak, it would make you *hate* me!

DION. What could you have done to make me hate you?

JUL. Do not ask me!

DION. Is it then such a secret?

JUL. Yes! And should you know it, I should lose the last prop of my strength and courage, Dionysia—my love! [*Embraces her. Enter Blangin*]

BLAN. Madam, your time's up. Prisoner, your counsel, M. Folgat and M. Magloire, awaits you. [*Exit. Jules gazes into Dionysia's face and smiles sadly*]

DION. You smile, Jules. You must have hope.

JUL. Yes, we all have hope! A crime has been committed, lives lost, Valpinson laid in ashes, the Count Clairnot fired upon! I am innocent! I swear it! I know the assassin! The world bids me speak—and yet, to speak would but proclaim me an accomplice and lead me to the guillotine!

DION. No, no! It must not—shall not be!

JUL. But how?

DION. [*Looking around. Then in a whisper*] You must escape!

JUL. Escape!

DION. Yes. Nothing easier! We have gold and can bribe your jailors. They will open the doors for you. In four hours you can reach Rochelle. Then a pilot boat will take you to England. Once there you are free! Jules de Dardeville, you are free!

JUL. And abandon you?

DION. No! I will follow you!

JUL. You would follow me?

DION. Yes! Do you think me base enough to abandon you, when all the world betrays you? No! We will meet in England. There we will change our name—go to some distant country. Once there, we shall be happy, happy!

JUL. [*Overcome*] Dionysia!

DION. [*Quickly*] Let us fix the day.

JUL. The day?

DION. Yes. The day for our flight.

JUL. The dream is too beautiful! [*After a pause*] No, Dionysia! No, I must not escape!

DION. You refuse me then, when I will join you and share your exile? Do you doubt my word? How can I bend you? What must I say? For my sake, if not for your own, let us fly! You escape disgrace! You secure liberty! Can nothing move you? What do you want? Must I throw myself at your feet?

JUL. I am innocent! To escape would be to confess that I am guilty!

DION. [*Clasping her hands over head, exclaims hopelessly*] I can say no more! I can say no more! [*Going up slowly, sobbing*]

JUL. [*Looking tearfully towards her, exclaims hysterically*] Dionysia! [*They embrace. He kisses her, then disengages her, and goes slowly towards seat near table*]

DION. [*Goes slowly up to door, stops, looks towards Jules*] Good-bye! Good-bye! [*Exits*]

JUL. [*Sinking in seat*] Good-bye! [*Then starting up*] No, no! To escape would be easy, but what then? To be a refugee trembling, day and night, lest a confessed murderer and incendiary should be detected! No, no! My dungeon walls would be a Heaven to such a life as that! Here I can sleep in quiet consciousness that I am innocent. Yes! I'll meet my fate and defend my honor to the last! [*Enter Blangin*]

BLAN. Prisoner, your counsel. [*Enter Folgat and Magloire. Jules receives them. Aside, down right*] A wonderful little woman, that Miss Dionysia! When I says here are the lawyers, ma'am, coming to hear what he has to say, says she to me, slipping me a whole napoleon, says she, "Let me hear what he says to the lawyers and I make it a hundred." [*Scratching his head*] Blangin, there's money in this case for you! [*Goes up and exits*]

FOL. Why, Jules, my boy, what a change has come over you!

MAG. Never fear, it will be all right. The commitment has not been made out. An alibi will free you tomorrow.

JUL. An alibi? That, my friends, I cannot prove. [*Dionysia appears at window-bars*]

FOL. and MAG. What?

JUL. An alibi, I cannot prove. For I was there.

FOL. and MAG. You were there?

JUL. Yes. Though, nevertheless, I am innocent.

FOL. Yet the world, even the Countess, believes you guilty.

JUL. [*Surprised*] The Countess Clairnot?

FOL. Yes, the Countess Clairnot! She has publicly and positively denounced you as the incendiary and assassin and demands justice!

JUL. [*Aside*] Traitress!

MAG. How do you explain it?

JUL. In a word—I was the *lover* of the Countess Clairnot!

DION. [*Aside*] Lover of the Countess Clairnot!

MAG. That is improbable!

FOL. Absurd!

JUL. Yes, but nevertheless the truth!

MAG. Are there any proofs of the fact?

JUL. None. We destroyed the letters a few moments before the fire.

FOL. Then you were at Valpinson a few minutes previous to the fire?

JUL. Yes.

FOL. If so, you probably may have heard or seen something to raise a suspicion in your mind as to who really was the incendiary?

JUL. I did.

FOL. Who?

JUL. The Countess Clairnot.

DION. [*Starts*] Ah!

FOL. and MAG. The Countess?

JUL. Yes. Her unjust accusation compels me to the confession. Had she never denounced me, knowing me to be innocent, I would have remained silent forever.

MAG. Speak! Who fired upon the Count?

JUL. Herself. [*General movement*]

MAG. But her object?

FOL. Yes, what could have been her object?

JUL. [*Bitterly*] To get rid of her husband, so that she could be free to claim her lover.

FOL. Did you see her in the act?

JUL. Is it likely that I would be accessory to such an act?

FOL. No! And yet you confess to having been a partner in the cause that impelled her to the crime—this secret and criminal alliance between herself and you. State to us the facts of the interview.

JUL. We had met at Valpinson, for the purpose of destroying our correspondence. She was very angry. I gave as a reason for my action that she was married and could never be mine. She asked me excitedly if I would have married her, had she been free. And to appease her, I weakly answered yes. Then she exclaimed "Oh, God! Luckily that thought never entered my brain before! Murder!" We parted. Shortly afterwards I heard a couple of shots. I thought it was poachers in the forest of Rochpommier and, looking back, beheld a conflagration. I thought it was the cathedral—then, the village. I hurried home, was arrested today, and charged with the crime!

MAG. To expose this assignation at Valpinson would avail you nothing.

FOL. No! It would, on the contrary, prove a motive for the crime, and be a confession that you were her accomplice.

MAG. Better keep the secret.

FOL. It is plain, that unless she confesses her entire guilt and, at the same time, avows your innocence—Jules de Dardeville, there is no escape for you!

JUL. That she will never do!

DION. [*Aside*] But she shall! And to me—and to me! [*Disappears from window*]

MAG. [*To Folgat*] Why not one of us visit her and question her?

FOL. Right! I, or Magloire, shall go tomorrow and, if we do not succeed—

JUL. Then I will go myself!

FOL. But how?

JUL. How? I have a fortune! What is that to life, liberty and honor? Gold shall purchase me the freedom of a night. And, if she has concluded to sacrifice me for her crime, in the presence of her husband, I will brand her with infamy!

FOL. Jules, my boy, this is terrible!

JUL. It is indeed! But I place my trust in Providence! Tell me—my father—my mother—do they believe me guilty?

FOL. No. They still have faith in a de Dardeville and, should all the world abandon you, believe you innocent.

DION. [*Appears at door*] And so would I!

JUL. [*Surprised*] Dionysia! Still here?

DION. Yes! I could not rest, knowing that you kept a secret so terrible in its character as to close your lips even to me. I listened there at the bars and, now that I know all—have heard all—I have come to forgive you. For I believe you innocent and, more than ever, I love you still! [*They embrace*]

ACT IV.

SCENE: *Chamber salon in the château of Count Clairnot. Doors R. and L.3.E. Large C. windows overlooking garden. Windows curtained. Large massive fireplace L.2.E. with fire. The whole appearance of the room elegant and massive. Large armchair L. Sofa R. Other articles of furniture around the room. Collette discovered arranging furniture, etc.*

COL. [*Coming C.*] Oh, how dreadful! How terrible! The Count Clairnot given up by the doctor and little Bertha dying! Yet madame, herself, goes about attending to everything just as calm, as cool and as kind as an angel! Ah, what a wonderful woman! [*Enter Dr. Seignebos L.3.E., coming down, unobserved by Collette and slapping her on the back*]

DR. S. Well, I'm going.

COL. [*With a startled scream*] How you frightened me!

DR. S. I say I'm going.

COL. Any one can tell that.

DR. S. Fudge!

COL. Indeed they can! Whether you are going or coming, you do everything with such a fuss and such a bounce that, really, I sometimes think it's an earthquake.

DR. S. What a girl—what a girl!

COL. How has the Count slept?

DR. S. Hasn't slept a wink. And as for poor little Bertha, she's wasted to a skeleton! I don't think she'll last much longer.

COL. And to think of all these dreadful things happening at once!

DR. S. Fate! [*Shaking his head*] But bad—bad! I've done all I can for them. There is no hope, Collette, no hope! [*Abruptly*] The Countess—how does she bear up?

COL. Ah, poor madame, she watches like an angel! She never leaves them. I don't think she has touched food, or closed her eyes, since the fire.

DR. S. [*Moved*] Poor Countess—poor Countess! I pity her! Pity her! [*Suddenly*] Well, I'm going. [*Slaps his hands, then slaps Collette on the shoulder*] Good-night. [*Exits quickly R.3.E.*]

COL. Bless me! He nearly broke my back! [*She turns down the gas. The moonlight falls through windows and illuminates the room*] I never saw such a man—comes and goes like a whirlpool—whirlwind—I mean. [*Going towards door R.3.E. Jules suddenly appears at door. Collette starts back and screams slightly*]

JUL. Silence! Is the Countess Clairnot in?

COL. The Countess cannot see anyone.

JUL. Cannot? Where is she? [*Coming down*]

COL. She's with her husband and her child. They are both very ill.

JUL. I must see her.

COL. Impossible!

JUL. Tell her that a gentleman who has been sent by Galpin, the prosecutor of Jules de Dardeville, desires to see her for a moment.

COL. Sent by Galpin, the prosecutor of the assassin! Certainly. Take a seat [*Points to sofa*] if you please, sir—and I'll tell her immediately. [*Exits R.3.E.*]

JUL. Ah, Countess Clairnot, we did not part forever! Fate brings us face to face once more! [*Places himself behind curtain C. Enter Countess Clairnot, hurriedly, L.3.E.*]

COUNTESS. A gentleman from M. Galpin to see me! Who can it be? [*Looking around*] I see no one. [*Jules steps from behind curtains*]

JUL. At last!

COUNTESS. [*Frightened*] Ah! [*Recognizing him*] Jules de Dardeville! [*She starts to door L. Jules quickly closes it and places himself before it*]

JUL. Stay, madam! Do not attempt to escape me. For if you do, I will pursue you to the very bedside of your husband!

COUNTESS. You—you, here! [*Leans against armchair L.*]

JUL. Yes, I am here. You are astonished, are you? You thought I was in prison, safe under lock and key. You said to yourself "No evidence can be found. Jules dare not speak. I have committed the crime. He will be punished for it! I am guilty, but I shall escape! He is innocent—yet he shall be sacrificed!" Is it not so? Speak! Is it not so?

COUNTESS. [*Alarmed*] I do not understand—

JUL. How I am here? Well, gold has purchased me the freedom of an hour. And I have come to brand you with the crime for which you would send me to the galleys.

COUNTESS. This is monstrous!

JUL. Aye! Monstrous, indeed!

COUNTESS. Murderer! Incendiary!

JUL. [*Laughs*] Ha! Ha! Ha! And *you—you* call *me* so?

COUNTESS. Yes! Yes! *I* call you so! You cannot deny your crime to me. I know the motives which the authorities do not even guess. You thought I would carry out my threat and you were frightened!

JUL. Frightened?

COUNTESS. Yes, frightened! All your promises and protestations were false —false as you are! You thought to yourself "Poor deluded woman—if I can but prevail upon her to destroy those letters, all proofs of our past intimacy will be ended! I'll then be free—*free* to marry this Dionysia Chandore! She will confess all to her husband! I will prevent that!" Aha! You see, you cannot deceive me! You kindled that fire in order to draw my husband out of the house. You incendiary! And then fired at him! You coward! [*Count appears at door L.3.E. He is very pale*]

JUL. Ha! Ha! Ha! Ha! And this is *your* plan? Who will believe this absurd story? Our letters were burnt. And, if you deny having been my mistress, I can just as well deny having been your lover. And, as to my being afraid of the Count Clairnot, your husband, it is well known that I am afraid of no one. When we were concealing our loves, at our secret place of meeting, I might have been afraid. For, had he surprised us there and availed himself of that just and righteous law which makes the husband both judge and executioner of his own case, [*The Count with fierce determination raises his pistol*] he could have shot me down like a dog. [*Count about to shoot*] Or, as I had tarnished his honor, he could abide his time to stain mine and avenge himself. [*Count, with a cry, lowers his pistol*] Except for this, what cared I for the Count Clairnot? What cared I for your threats or his hatred?

COUNTESS. If you are innocent, who, then, could be guilty?

JUL. [*Seizes both her hands and hisses in her ear*] You! Wretched woman —you!

COUNTESS. [*With a cry of horror*] Me? Great Heaven!

JUL. You wanted to be free that you might prevent me from breaking the chains in which you held me. At our last meeting, when I thought you were crushed by grief, and was softened by your hypocritical tears—your anger, which I mistook for love—I was weak enough to say "I marry Dionysia only because you are not free." Then you cried "Oh, God! How lucky it is that thought never entered my brain before!" What thought? Come! Answer me! Confess!

COUNTESS. Confess?

JUL. Aye! That thought was murder!

COUNTESS. I was mad—mad—I tell you, with jealousy and anger! I have outraged and destroyed my husband's honor! But to murder him! Bah! You accuse me of what you know to be a lie!

JUL. Then, madam, as you say—if you are innocent, who could be guilty? [*Countess sinks in chair with horror*]

JUL. [*Bitterly*] You act your part well!

COUNTESS. You believe I am the guilty one?

JUL. [*Ironically*] Perhaps you only planned the crime and ordered some one else to execute it.

COUNTESS. Great Heavens! [*They stand for a few moments staring at each other silently*] Well, sir, what is to be done?

JUL. The truth must be told.

COUNTESS. Which truth?

JUL. That I have been your lover; that I went to Valpinson, by appointment with you; that I came for the purpose of destroying our letters; and that the cartridge found there was accidentally dropped by me when I drew your letters from my pocket.

COUNTESS. You want me to say this?

JUL. Yes.

COUNTESS. You want me to bear half the guilt?

JUL. The truth must be told.

COUNTESS. Never!

JUL. It shall be told!

COUNTESS. Never! Never! Do you not see that the truth cannot be told—that it would prove that we were accomplices and convict us both?

JUL. Never mind. I am not willing to die.

COUNTESS. Rather say, that you do not want to die alone—that you want to drag me down with you!

JUL. Be it so.

COUNTESS. To confess, would be to ruin me! Is that what you want? Would your fate be less cruel if there were two victims instead of one?

JUL. You calculate—you bargain!

COUNTESS. Yes. Because I love you. Remember, Jules, you are the father of my child. [*Drawing closely to him, her voice losing its intensity and speaking in a soft, pleading way*] One word from you, and I leave them all! Country, friends, husband, *child!* Speak that word, Jules, and I follow you, without turning my head, without a regret, without a tear. Why do you hesitate? Do you not see that I cannot part from you? Why, man, man, do you not see that I am ready to sacrifice my very soul for you? [*She throws herself at his feet*] Speak! Speak! [*Jules throws her off. She reels and falls on sofa R.*]

JUL. No! No! [*Following her*] Murderess! Rather the scaffold! [*Pause*]

COUNTESS. [*Recovering and speaking slowly*] *Then what do you want of me?*

JUL. The truth.

COUNTESS. To what purpose? [*Jules turns from her*] That you may be free to marry Dionysia Chandore! I am the past to you! She is the future! The old love must be made a footstool for the new! I must be disgraced, that she be honored! I must weep, that she may smile! No! No! [Note: *The actor playing the Count is the best creator of his business and by-play during this scene*]

JUL. Wretch!

COUNTESS. [*Savagely*] You do not know me yet! You shall never be hers! You belong either to the scaffold or to me! Either your life, or my love! [*Holding out her hands in supplication*]

JUL. We shall see! [*Starts towards door L.3.E.*]

COUNTESS. Where would you go?

JUL. To your husband.

COUNTESS. [*Defiantly*] Go! Speak! Denounce me! M. Folgat no doubt has told you how well I can defend myself. Your word would not be worth that! [*Snaps her fingers defiantly*]

JUL. Fiend! [*Rushes towards her as though to strike her. The Count comes C. from his place of concealment*]

COUNT. Do not strike that woman! [*Pointing pistol*]

JUL. The Count!

COUNTESS. My husband!

COUNT. I have heard all! [*Looking at them both with disgust and scorn*] Miserable wretches! [*Countess sinks into armchair L.*]

JUL. I have insulted you, sir. Avenge yourself!

COUNT. [*With a cold, hard laugh, lowering his pistol*] No, no! The law will avenge me.

JUL. What! Would you permit me to be condemned for a crime of which I am innocent? Ah! That would be cowardly!

COUNT. [*Supporting himself by back of chair*] Cowardly? What do you call the act of him who, meanly, disgracefully, robs another of his wife, and palms his own child upon him? What is the fire in my house compared with the ruin of my faith? What are the wounds in my body in comparison with that in my heart? Go! Go! Miserable wretch! You cannot escape! I leave you to the law!

JUL. Rather death, death! [*Baring his breast*] Why do you not fire? Are you afraid of blood? Shoot! I have been the lover of your wife! Your daughter is my child! [*Count with a cry of rage, raises his pistol*] Kill me and avenge your honor!

COUNT. [*Lowering pistol*] No! The arm of the law is more certain than mine—its aim more unerring!

JUL. [*In despair*] You will not kill me?

COUNT. No! Remember your own words, "As I had tarnished his honor, he could abide his time to stain mine and avenge himself."

JUL. My God!

COUNT. Now you know why I will not kill you. You have robbed me of my honor and I must have yours. And, if you cannot be condemned without it, in my dying deposition I shall say—I shall swear—that I recognized you as the assassin. [*With a cry of horror, Jules crouches on sofa R. Countess stands as immovable as a statue L. Count, overcome with passion, stands with almost superhuman strength, then totters and falls*]

ACT V.

SCENE: *Elegant salon in the château of the Countess Clairnot. C. doors. Door R.3.E. Large bay-window opening on porch L. Fireplace R.2.E. Elegant furniture and decorations in room. Armchair R.1.E. Armchair L.2.E. Sofa L., etc. Collette discovered on porch, arranging flowers, etc. Dr. Seignebos enters R.3.E.*

DR. S. [*Loudly*] Well?

COL. [*Startled*] Oh! [*Coming forward*] Goodness, how you startled me! I thought the roof had fallen in!

DR. S. [*Feeling her pulse*] Nervousness! Nervousness!

COL. No, sir! Allow me to say I am not nervous. I have courage enough to stand anything in reason.

DR. S. Fudge! How is the Countess since yesterday?

COL. Very quiet, sir.

DR. S. And little Bertha?

COL. Worse than when you left her.

DR. S. I am afraid she will soon follow her father.

COL. Poor Count!

DR. S. Where did you find him the night he died?

COL. In the library, pale and rigid, his features fearfully distorted. He was unconscious and never spoke.

Dr. S.[3] He became delirious, no doubt, with fever brought on by his wounds and, wandering from his apartment, his bandages came off, occasioning his immediate death.

Col. Poor master! Poor master!

Dr. S. Yes, yes! [*Abruptly, but very quiet*] Now then, Collette, I will attend to Bertha. [*Exits C. and L.*]

Col. [*Surprised*] Why, what has come over the doctor? I never saw him go out so quiet before! [*Dionysia appears at door R.3.E. Turning and seeing her*] Madame—

Dion. [*Coming down*] Is your mistress in?

Col. Yes, madame.

Dion. Tell her a lady wishes to see her.

Col. [*Going, then stops*] Shall I say whom, madame?

Dion. It is unnecessary. Merely say that it is important. [*Collette bows and exits C. and L.*]

Dion. Yes, I shall speak to her! I shall ask her how she dares to rob him of life and honor, knowing him to be innocent and herself the criminal! He is innocent! He is innocent! And if I cannot move her to pity they will murder him! His best friends acknowledge him no longer! No hand will grasp his! And even those who were most proud of his friendship pretend to have forgotten his name! Great Heaven! And they call this human justice! But she can save him! She can save him! But will she—will she? [*Collette re-enters C. and L.*]

Col. Madame, the Countess sends word she cannot see you.

Dion. Cannot? She must! She shall! Go back. Tell the Countess that it is *I*, Dionysia Chandore! That if she does not come to me, I shall go to her. That I will arouse the neighborhood and publicly accuse her of the infamy for which another now innocently suffers!

Col. But madame—

Dion. Go. [*Pointing*] It is a question of life and death! [*Collette bows and exits*] Yes, of life and death! And all depends on me, on me! But if I fail? Fail! I cannot—I must not fail! [*Enter Countess C., pale but very calm*]

Countess. Since you insist upon it, madame, I have come to tell you myself that I cannot listen to you. Are you not aware that I am standing near the grave of my poor child? [*Going*]

Dion. If you leave me without listening to me, I will follow you and shall speak in the presence of the dying.

Countess. Indeed! Is your business of so much importance then?

[3] This speech is crossed out in the manuscript and was evidently omitted in the acting version.

DION. [*Tearfully*] It is, madame.

COUNTESS. [*Immovable*] Then be seated. [*Dionysia sits R. Countess sits L.*] Proceed. I hear you.

DION. It is unnecessary to tell you my name.

COUNTESS. It is. I know! [*Half looking up*] You are Dionysia Chandore.

DION. You know that Jules de Dardeville has been put on his trial?

COUNTESS. I do.

DION. And that you—you—can save him—

COUNTESS. [*Calmly looking up*] I?

DION. You seemed surprised, madame.

COUNTESS. And why should I not be? What do I know of Jules de Dardeville? How could I save him?

DION. He asserts that you know a great deal. Your past intimacy—

COUNTESS. [*Affecting great surprise*] My past intimacy?

DION. Yes. He states that he left you only a few moments before the fire took place—that you know his innocence and can prove it.

COUNTESS. [*Starting up*] This is infamous! Infamous! What? Jules de Dardeville has dared to tell you that?

DION. Do not misunderstand me. Jules de Dardeville was your lover. He deserted you. You would now have your revenge by making him suffer for a crime of which he is innocent!

COUNTESS. Innocent? Has he the audacity to assert this? Has he the audacity to charge me with having been his mistress? And to *you?*

DION. No. He told me nothing. He simply confided it to his counsel. I listened and overheard all!

COUNTESS. Then what do you want of me?

DION. To testify in his behalf—to confess enough to save him!

COUNTESS. To confess *enough?* I do not understand you!

DION. Yes, you do understand me, madame. Why will you deny it? Do you not see that I know all?

COUNTESS. [*Controlling herself*] Oh, this is too much! This is too much!

DION. Can you not see that his love for you has brought him to destruction? That he suffers wrongfully and you stand coldly by? Oh, what a woman you must be, not to cry out in open court and proclaim his innocence! How can you live and see the man you love go down to shame and infamy?

COUNTESS. [*Rising*] No, no! It is not so! Only a week ago, he came here and I offered to fly with him. He had only to say the word and I would have given up everything for him!

DION. [*Quickly*] And he answered?

COUNTESS. Rather the scaffold! [*Approaching her*] Did this look as though I cared to see him go to shame and infamy? He refused me! He condemned himself! [*Dionysia sinks down, burying her face in her hands. Over her*] I was quite willing to ruin myself for him. But I am certainly not willing to do so for another woman!

DION. [*Supplicating*] Pity!

COUNTESS. For you? *You,* for whose sake he abandoned me! *You,* whom he was going to marry! *You,* with whom he hoped to enjoy long, happy years!

DION. Pity! Pity!

COUNTESS. [*Through her teeth*] To you? *You,* to whom I owe all my misery and sorrow?

DION. Not for me—for him! I have come to offer you a bargain.

COUNTESS. [*Recovering herself*] A bargain? What bargain can *you* have to offer *me?*

DION. Save Jules and, by all that is sacred to me in the world, I promise that I will enter a convent! I will renounce the world and you shall never hear of me again.

COUNTESS. [*Seated L., ironically*] You would really do that?

DION. Unhesitatingly!

COUNTESS. *You* would make this great sacrifice for me?

DION. For you—for Jules!

COUNTESS. You love him then so dearly, do you?

DION. I love him dearly enough to prefer his happiness a thousand times to my own! Even when buried in a convent, I should have the consolation of knowing I had saved him.

COUNTESS. And would this make him love me? No! You know that he loves you alone. Heroism with such conditions is easy enough! What have you to fear? Buried in a convent, he would love you none the less, and hate me all the more!

DION. But he shall never know—

COUNTESS. What would that matter? He loves me no longer. My love, to him, is a heavier load than the cannonball that's fastened to his chains!

DION. [*In despair*] Oh, this is horrible!

COUNTESS. [*With force*] Horrible? Yes! [*Dionysia looks up*] You look amazed! You have, as yet, only seen the morning of your love. Wait till the dark evening comes on! Then you will understand me—

DION. [*Pleading*] Oh, pity me, madame, pity me! [*Falls on sofa*]

COUNTESS. [*Following her up*] Our stories are the same. I have seen Jules at my feet. *You* have him now at yours. The vows of love he swore to me, he now swears to *you*. You *have* his promises—so *had* I!

DION. Oh, madame, spare me—spare me!

COUNTESS. But you think you will be his wife? And I never was! What does that matter? What does he tell you? That he will love you forever, because his love is under the protection of God and man? He told me, because our love was not thus protected, that we should be united by an indissoluble bond—a bond stronger than all others—Death! You have his promise! So have I! It is time for one of us to claim it.

DION. [*Overcome, falls at her feet*] My God! Mercy! Mercy! No more!

COUNTESS. You—you have sacrificed nothing for him—I, everything—the world! I gave him all and, if there had been more to give, he should have had it! Aye, even my very soul! And now, to be betrayed, forsaken, despised! And then to allow myself to be moved by your tears! No, no! Do not think I'll let the vengeance I hold in my hands slip from me at your bidding! Go! Go! [*Pointing*] Expect nothing from me.

DION. No, no, I cannot go! I will not go, till you proclaim his innocence. Save him! Save him! [*At her feet*] Here at your feet, I beg, I implore, I supplicate, for mercy! Save him! My God! Would you see me die? Would you see me go mad—mad? [*Dionysia drags herself up to Countess. Countess throws her off. Dionysia falls and catches back of armchair L. and supports herself*]

COUNTESS. Girl, girl, you plead in vain! Let him expiate his crime by the law. He is an incendiary, a murderer!

DION. [*Suddenly raising herself upright and turning to the Countess*] Countess Clairnot, you lie!

COUNTESS. [*Triumphantly*] Who then is?

DION. You! Murderess! You!

COUNTESS. [*Starts, clutches back of chair R.*] Me? Have a care! Have a care!

DION. Oh, I fear you no longer! I supplicate no longer! We have proof! Absolute, overwhelming proof!

COUNTESS. [*Laughs*] Then produce your proof! We shall see if the vile calumnies of an incendiary can stain the reputation of an honest woman!

DION. [*Mockingly*] An honest woman!

COUNTESS. Yes. We shall see if a single speck of this mud in which you wallow can reach up to me! Go! Go, I tell you!

DION. [*Rushing to Countess*] Woman, woman, you must! You shall! [*Collette enters quickly C.*]

COL. Madame, little Bertha is sinking fast, and asks for you.

COUNTESS. [*With great impatience, waving her off fiercely*] In a moment! In a moment! Go! [*Exit Collette*]

COUNTESS. [*Turning to Dionysia*] I *must,* I *shall,* what?

DION. Save Jules's life!

COUNTESS. [*Through her teeth*] Never! Never!

DION. By the memory of your dying child, in its name, in its love, forgive Jules—forgive me—and save him!

COUNTESS. [*Throwing her off*] Never! Never! Never! [*Enter Dr. Seignebos and Collette C.*]

DR. S. Madame, your child is dead.

COUNTESS. [*Stunned*] Dead? Dead! [*Pause*] The last tie that bound me to him is severed. My life has passed away! My heart is stone! Go, go to your lover, girl, and tell him this for me—that the Countess Clairnot confesses before these witnesses that she was the assassin of her husband, and Jules de Dardeville her accomplice. [*Dionysia shrieks and falls*]

ACT VI.

SCENE: *Reception room in the prison of Sauveterre. C. doors opening on corridor and view of a portion of prison. Large marble steps leading to room. Door R.3.E. with steps. Door L.2.E. leading to private room. Grated window L. Chant heard as curtain rises. Prison bell strikes seven. Blangin discovered looking off C. towards L.*

BLAN. Another hour and Jules de Dardeville will be no more. [*Enter Dr. Seignebos R.3.E. He comes down steps and approaches Blangin, unobserved*]

DR. S. [*Loud and suddenly*] Well?

BLAN. [*Starting*] The devil! I thought the prisoner had escaped!

DR. S. Fudge! [*Aside*] I wish he had!

BLAN. But he's all right. His death will be painless.

DR. S. How do you know? Did you ever try it?

BLAN. Me? No, I never had that pleasure. [*Noise of hammering heard off L.*]

DR. S. What's that?

BLAN. Oh, they're only putting up the scaffold.

DR. S. *Only?* Does the prisoner hear it?

BLAN. Certainly. It must be a great consolation for him to know his troubles will soon be over.

DR. S. *Great* consolation indeed!

BLAN. It was an awful crime, sir, and the prisoner deserves his fate.

DR. S. [*Aside*] Deserves a fiddlestick!

BLAN. The poor Countess has never recovered from the shock.

DR. S. No! Nor perhaps she never will. I was at her house the night she lost her wits.

BLAN. [*Interested*] Tell me about it.

DR. S. It was caused by overexcitement. The condemned's betrothed had called to ask the Countess to intercede in his behalf. The previous events—the fire—the death of her husband—followed so suddenly by that of her child—all combined, were too much for her mind to bear. She became delirious, hysterical, actually insane, began to rave, and declared herself the assassin of her husband, and Jules de Dardeville only her accomplice!

BLAN. Ridiculous!

DR. S. Yes. No notice was taken of her ravings, for we all knew she was *non compos mentis*.

BLAN. Poor woman!

DR. S. She hasn't recovered from the shock since. The only thing that interests her is the trial and conviction of Jules de Dardeville.

BLAN. [*Looking off L.*] Hush! Here is the magistrate. [*Enter Galpin and Seneschal R.3.E. and come down steps*]

GAL. [*Bows stiffly to Doctor, then turns to Blangin*] How has the prisoner spent the night?

BLAN. Very quietly, sir.

GAL. Are the good fathers with him still?

BLAN. Yes, sir.

GAL. He is reconciled, then, to meet his fate?

BLAN. Yes. So I heard him tell them.

GAL. That will do. [*Blangin bows and exits C. off L.*]

DR. S. [*Crossing to Galpin, ironically*] M. Galpin, allow me to compliment you upon your admirable prosecution of the case. You will no doubt some day become a very great man.

GAL. I did my duty, sir. Had he been my brother, it would have been all the same.

DR. S. [*Aside, going L.*] Yes, or your grandmother! [*Enter Folgat and Magloire R.3.E. Bows exchanged*]

FOL. [*To Galpin*] I was seeking you. Has the petition for delay been received?

GAL. No.

FOL. [*In despair*] No?

GAL. No! You may expect no mercy from the Emperor. The condemned was an avowed Republican.

FOL. There is then no hope?

GAL. None. [*Bell strikes one, a quarter past. To Blangin, who walks up and down corridor*] Admit the prisoner. [*Blangin exits L. Sound of unlocking prison bolts. Two Gendarmes enter and place themselves R. and L. of C. doors, followed by Jules de Dardeville. He is pale but very calm. Blangin continues his walk up and down the corridor. Jules comes down and grasps the hands of Folgat and Magloire, then the Doctor. He turns around and bows to Galpin and Seneschal*]

FOL. Ah, Jules, this is hard, very hard!

JUL. Bear up my friend! Do not unman me. I am innocent and can face death like a man. [*Grasping his hand*] You have done all that you could for me, but fate has ordained it otherwise. [*Turns to Magloire*] You, too, have been my friend. Good-bye! [*Magloire shakes hands with Jules, then retires up stage, greatly moved. To Doctor, who comes down*] Ah, Doctor, friendship's a word that's easily said, but you have proved a true friend indeed. [*Shakes his hand*] Farewell!

DR. S. [*Overcome*] Fif-fif-fer—well! [*Goes up, wiping his eyes with handkerchief*]

GAL. [*Crosses to Jules*] You will, I am sure, pardon me for the unpleasant part I have taken in your prosecution. You know law is law.

DR. S. [*Aside, at back*] D-da-damn the law!

JUL. M. Galpin, life is too short to waste in enmity. Standing, as I am, upon the verge of eternity, I would not deprive you of whatever satisfaction you may have in life. You have done your duty, such as you consider it! Farewell! [*Offers his hand*]

GAL. [*Taking it*] Farewell! [*Aside, going R.*] The greatest execution on the calendar! My fortune's made! [*Bell strikes two*]

JUL. [*Struggling with his feelings, overcomes them and continues calmly*] Now comes the worst of all. Dionysia. [*To Blangin*] Admit her. [*Blangin exits L.2.E. and enters immediately with Dionysia. She rushes to Jules. He opens his arms*] Dionysia!

DION. [*Sobbing*] Jules! Jules! [*Enter Countess Clairnot R.3.E. in deep mourning and heavily veiled. She remains at back unobserved*]

JUL. Dionysia, do not unman me.

DION. [*Sobs*] Oh, my heart, my heart is breaking!

JUL. Dionysia! Dionysia! Let me meet my fate calmly. See! I am not afraid. I never was more resigned to anything in my life. Nothing but the sight of your grief could unman me.

DION. Jules! Jules!

JUL. Your sweet and innocent love for me has turned and stung you like a serpent! If it were not for this, I could go to my grave without a pang, without a sorrow.

DION. Oh, Jules, Jules, would that I could die with you!

GAL. [*Coming to her*] Calm yourself. [*Dionysia turns away from him without noticing his remark*] I am the magistrate, yet I can sympathize.

DION. [*Turning to him*] *You—you* sympathize? Yes, as the serpent sympathizes with the victim it fascinates! He was your friend! In his noble and generous nature, he cherished you. Misfortune came and you turned upon him like a viper! May the memory of his headless corpse be to you an accursed phantom, hideous as the image of your own soul, cruel as your miserable ambition!

DR. S. [*At back, aside*] Bravo! Bravo!

GAL. [*Annoyed*] Were it not for the situation, miss, I should teach you to respect the magistrate, if you did not the man. [*Goes up. Bell strikes three*]

DION. [*Screams and clings to Jules*] Oh, Jules, Jules, must you die?

JUL. [*Embracing her quickly*] Dionysia! My love! My love! I cannot struggle! I cannot fight with fate! My end is drawing near. [*Kisses her, then disengages himself from her*] Farewell! Farewell! [*Dionysia, screaming, is taken from his arms by Folgat and led off L.2.E. Jules for the first time is overcome and bursts into tears, and sinks on chair L.*] This is terrible! Thank Heaven, I am spared another meeting with my parents!

GAL. [*Comes down and touches him on shoulder*] M. Jules de Dardeville, you have but a few moments left. Prepare yourself. [*Jules rises quickly and stands erect and calm. Folgat enters L.2.E.*]

JUL. [*To Folgat*] To you, I entrust my fortune, to be divided among such charitable institutions as you think fit. Comfort my poor parents—and—[*Mastering himself*]—and—Dionysia! Farewell! [*Turning to Galpin*] Sir, I am ready. [*They move up slowly to C. The Guard appears in corridor and stands in file. Enter Cocoleau, quickly, R.3.E. He is pale and wild looking, his eyes almost staring out of his head. He sees Countess, who comes down R. corner unobserved, as others move up C.*]

COUNTESS. [*Seeing him, seizes him by the arm and brings him to her*] The vial! Quick, Cocoleau! The vial!

COCO. [*Laughs*] He! He! He! Here it is. [*Takes it from his breast*] I found it just where you told me—in the little back drawer. I got it! I got it! Here it is. [*Gives it to her and, putting his hands to his head, laughs idiotically*]

COUNTESS. In life he has been mine! Death shall not part us. [*Snatches vial from Cocoleau and throws off her veil*] Jules de Dardeville, we die together! [*General movement*]

OMNES. Countess Clairnot!

COUNTESS. Aye! The Countess Clairnot! [*Raises the vial quickly, then starts*] It is empty! [*To Cocoleau*] Wretch! Fool! What have you done with the contents?

COCO. [*Almost reeling, places his hand to his head, and starts as if in great pain*] Done—with—contents? [*Laughs*] He! He! He! I drank it.

COUNTESS. You drank it?

COCO. [*Laughing and smiling knowingly*] Ye—yes!

COUNTESS. Idiot! You are poisoned!

OMNES. Poisoned?

COCO. [*Staggers C. and stands in great suffering, showing the symptoms of a poisoned man, and in spite of all, looking at Countess with an expression of profound love and devotion, smiles*] I—I—I know it.

COUNTESS. You knew it? And still you drank it? [*Characters all drop down, interested*]

COCO. [*Knowingly*] Ye—yes—for if I hadn't—*you* would—and—and—Cocoleau didn't want that! Cocoleau didn't want—that.

COUNTESS. [*Turns away*] Fool! [*Cocoleau reels and falls C.*]

GAL. [*Impatiently*] We are wasting time.

FOL. We still have five minutes. I crave your indulgence—

GAL. I regret it deeply, but—

FOL. The ravings of this idiot convicted my client. His ravings now may clear him. I *insist!*

GAL. [*Impatiently*] As you please.

FOL. [*Bows*] Thank you. [*Cocoleau recovering and looking in a sort of dazed manner, his eyes finally resting on the Countess, then on Jules. He then bursts into a flood of tears*] There is something he wants to tell.

DR. S. [*Going to Cocoleau*] He is sinking fast. In a few moments all will be over.

FOL. [*Kneeling by Cocoleau*] My boy, is there anything I can do for you?

COCO. [*Looking at him*] Ye—yes!

FOL. What? Speak.

COCO. Raise—raise me up! I—I—want—to say something.

FOL. [*Raises his head*] Now say it, my boy. [*Cocoleau turns and looks at Countess with expression of "May I?"*]

COUNTESS. Speak!

Coco. [*With effort*] Yes—I—want—to—say—it—so bad. [*To Countess*] You—won't—be angry—with—poor Cocoleau—will you? I—I—can't keep—it—any longer. I—I—must speak—or I—shall choke—choke! [*Tears open his collar; after a slight pause*] You—sent—me for the poison. You—wanted to—drink it—because—you—were so—unhappy—and—when—you—were—unhappy—Cocoleau was—unhappy too! I love you—I love you—oh, so much! You—wanted—to—drink it—because—he—he—[*Pointing to Jules*]—was—going to die—and you—wanted—to die—with him! [*Laughs*] But I—can save—him! I can—save—him! And—you can live—live—and poor Cocoleau—will die for—both—both! [*Falls back*]

Fol. Go on, my boy! Go on!

Dr. S. Hush!

Coco. [*After effort, painfully*] He—he—[*Pointing to Jules*] didn't—kill master. No—no—no! [*Laughs idiotically*]

Fol. No? Then who did?

Coco. [*Triumphantly*] I—I—I! [*Laughs. Magloire exits L.2.E. and enters immediately with Dionysia. Dionysia, with a cry, rushes to Jules*]

Countess. You?

Jul. You?

Omnes. You? [*Countess and Jules stare at each other*]

Coco. Yes—I—shot—Count Clairnot—and—Jules—de—Dardeville—is—innocent!

Gal. *You* shot Count Clairnot? Why?

Coco. [*Crawling to feet of Countess and kissing her dress*] To—to please—my pretty lady. [*Looking up in her face with the love and devotion of a dog*] She loved—him—[*Pointing to Jules*] and—she—didn't love—the Count! She—she used—to cry—much—much—to herself—and say—if she—was free—Jules de Dardeville would—marry her. She was—always—so good—and—kind—to—poor Cocoleau—and Cocoleau—loved her—loved her—and puzzled—his poor—brain—[*Feels his burning temples*] to find out—how he—could—save her. So—when—he—came—the—night of—the fire—I was—hid—in—the shrubbery—and—heard what—they said. And—when—he burnt the letters—I threw—them under—the house with—some—shavings—just to—draw—master out. [*Looking up*] It—was—not—my fault if the—whole house—went afire. And—when—master came—out—I shot—him! [*Sinks back exhausted*]

Countess. [*Aside*] Jules de Dardeville innocent!

Jul. [*Aside*] She, guiltless!

GAL. This confession, to have weight, must be corroborated by something more than a simple self-accusation. The law is very clear on this point. [*To Cocoleau, as he slowly raises himself up*] Have you anything more to say? [*Cocoleau shakes his head painfully*]

FOL. Can you think of nothing? [*Cocoleau shakes his head. Suddenly*] The weapon? What did you do with the weapon?

COCO. [*After effort*] The gun—the gun—[*Suddenly remembering*] Ah! It's there—there—under—the steps—of the prison. I hid—it—there—last night. [*Folgat exits quickly R.3.E. Delirious, crawling to Countess*] Good-bye—good-bye! Don't curse poor Cocoleau. He did—it—all for you—all—for—you—dear—dear—lady! [*Dies. During the last of Cocoleau's death scene, he rises and staggers towards L.2.E. and when he dies, he is caught in the arms of two Gendarmes and dragged off L.2.E. Enter Folgat with gun. He hands it to Galpin*]

GAL. [*Takes gun and examines it*] Yes, this was the property of the Count Clairnot. His name is on the stock. It now rests on the Countess Clairnot to substantiate the dying statement of Cocoleau. [*All eyes are turned on the Countess Clairnot. To Jules*] Your life is in her hands. It is a trying moment. For her honor, her reputation hangs in the balance.

JUL.[5] What will she do? [*Pause*]

COUNTESS. [*Slowly, without raising her eyes*] Jules de Dardeville, innocent myself, I believed you guilty. I *hated* her. I *hated* her so, that I could have seen you expiate the crime with which you were charged with joy. Had I known you to be innocent, I should have spoken before this. I do not ask forgiveness. I do not even want your pity. You have wronged me more deeply than I have wronged you. Your wound will heal. Mine never will—for it has left its poison here! [*Clasps her hand over her heart and turns away for a second, deeply affected*]

JUL.[6] Genevieve—for her sake—

COUNTESS. What little reparation I can make, I make to her. [*To Dionysia*] You are too good and noble, your love too innocent and pure, to be shadowed by the darkness that broods over mine. My sacrifice is great, very great—for it leaves me nothing—not even my good name. [*Turning to Galpin*] M. Galpin, what M. Jules de Dardeville has stated before is true, every word of it. [*To Dionysia*] Forgive me!

DION. [*Goes and kisses Countess*] Freely.

[5] This speech was added to the manuscript in revision in Herne's handwriting.
[6] This speech was also added to the manuscript in revision in Herne's handwriting.

COUNTESS. [*Patting her head*] He loves you, and you were ready to sacrifice your life for his sake! He forsakes me, but I sacrificed my name, my honor, for him. Farewell! Jules! [*Jules embraces Dionysia*] Let my great and overwhelming love for you be my excuse. [*Kisses his hand*] Farewell! You will never see me again. [*Turns to Dionysia*] From my convent cell I will pray that you may be happy! God bless you! [*Overcome, covers her face with her hands. Jules kisses Dionysia. Bell strikes eight*]

CURTAIN

"THE MINUTE MEN"
OF
1774-1775

CAST OF CHARACTERS

[*Chestnut Street Theatre, Philadelphia, April 6, 1886*]

SIR FREDERICK SHELTON, *Colonel in His Majesty's 18th British Grenadiers*	HENRY TALBOT
CAPTAIN HENRY WINSLOW, *Retired officer of the old French War*	THOMAS J. HERNDON
REUBEN FOXGLOVE, *"Minute Man"*	JAMES A. HERNE
NED FARNSWORTH, *Captain of the Minute Men*	CHARLES G. CRAIG
ROANOKE, *An Indian*	CHARLES W. VANDENHOFF
DYKE HAMPTON, *Cousin of, and affianced to Rachel*	M. J. JORDAN
MORTON HANDY, *In service of Hampton*	J. C. WALSH
LIEUTENANT SMOLLET, *Of the 18th Grenadiers*	HARRY M. PITT
DOROTHY FOXGLOVE, *Adopted daughter of Reuben*	KATHARINE CORCORAN
RACHEL WINSLOW, *Daughter of Captain Henry Winslow*	MARY WILKES
ANN CAMPBELL, *A woman of the period*	JENNIE REIFFERTH

JOE ALLEN } *Minute Men*
ROBERT HERRICK }

AN ORDERLY, *English*

A SERGEANT, *English*

COLONEL SMITH, *English*

MINUTE MEN, ENGLISH AND AMERICAN SOLDIERS, DRUMMERS, FIFERS, INDIANS, ETC., ETC.

ACT I.

TIME: *1774.*

SCENE I: *Dorchester Heights with Bay of Massachusetts seen in distance R.H. The scene at opening represents a summer afternoon after a heavy thunderstorm, and must have that grand effect the sun gives shining through a peculiar sky after a rain, rendering one portion of the scene nearly dark, the other lighted by a peculiar but very effective brightness—the entire effect very picturesque and true to history. During the Act the sun sets and twilight appears—the sky and entire scene must change with the setting sun. On the left is an old-fashioned farm house and dairy. The house is built after the manner of the better houses of its period—say 1740 or thereabouts: viz. logs or timbers so exactly squared and joined as to make smooth compact walls, has long low porch and low verandah, the whole neatly whitewashed; vines clamber over porch and flower garden surrounds the R.H. end and corner. Old-fashioned plow R.3.E. Rustic seat R. of dairy. Rustic chair down R. The dairy is open to the audience and contains churn of the period and dairy implements, all of which are scrupulously clean, a pail partly filled with clean water and a gourd for dipping it out. The R.H. is shrubbery and foliage—the back looking on to the arm and away to the Bay on the R. and distant hills on the L.H. Discovered: Ann Campbell in dairy churning. She is dressed in homespun old-fashioned gown, hair plainly done in style of time; is a good natured, determined woman. British Soldiers in fatigue dress are seen occasionally passing to and fro at back during scene, but paying no attention to dialogue or action. "Music" very bright and characteristic at rise—opens ff., becomes piano as curtain goes up and dies gradually away as Hampton speaks. Enter from U.E.R. Dyke Hampton, a dark, sinister man about forty-five years of age. He is dressed in riding habit of well-to-do man of period, carries a whip.*

DYKE. [*Speaking as he enters*] Good-day, Mrs. Campbell. I hope I see you well!

ANN. [*Looking up but not ceasing work and evincing no pleasure at seeing him*] Why, Mr. Hampton! Who'd a'thought a'seein' yeou, this day of all days!

DYKE. [*Coming towards dairy*] Well, you see, like the hunter in the chase, I thought I'd be in at the death! [*Music ceases*]

ANN. Yes! An' as Rachel writes, ef it hadn't a'been for the all merciful hand o'Providence, it might a'been in at the death indeed! [*Pours water into churn*]

DYKE. [*Taking seat R. of dairy*] The accident was serious then!

ANN. [*Churning*] Wa'll it wa'ant no jokin' matter—but where was yeou that yeou didn't know?

DYKE. Absent at York. Trying to recover some of my Hampshire land grants.

ANN. Ya'as—lands, some folks about here say you never lost!

DYKE. Indeed—who are the some folks—pray?

ANN. [*Looking at him curiously, then taking off churn cover, looking into churn, replacing cover and churning furiously*] I disremember they're names jist now; but you was atalkin' about the Captain and Rachel!

DYKE. Yes—I am anxious to obtain the particulars of the accident. Will you be good enough to relate them?

ANN. Sartin! Sartin! Unless you'd prefer to hear 'em from the lips of Rachel herself, which of course you've a right to, seein' as how you're engaged—eh? They say you be engaged! Be you?

DYKE. Pardon me, Mrs. Campbell, but will you oblige me with the information I came to seek?

ANN. Sartin! Sartin! Well, yeou see, about a month ago the Captain an' Rachel was a'returnin' hum from they're visit to Albany, when in descendin' a mountainious rud the hosses took fright an' gettin' the better of the Captain, who ain't as young as he was once, dashed down the mountain like all possessed. The carriage was overturned an' the Captain was purty badly shook up besides a' sprainin' of what he calls his fightin' leg—cos it wouldn't run away when the other one wanted to at the battle of Quebec—an'—

DYKE. Yes—yes—I know!

ANN. Exactly! Well, Rachel, she screams an' then faints—as any other brave woman'd a'done—an' out o' the forest comes a tall, handsome man—jist for all the world like a page out'n a story book, an' manages to carry 'em to his cabin nearby—an' bein' half hunter—half docter—good Samaritan, Balm O'Gillead an' ministerin' angel all rolled into one—he sets to work a'nussin' an' a'docterin' 'em with harbs an' simples till they're strong enough to resume journey hum, where if nothing further happens they'll all three arrive afore dusk!

DYKE. Oh! Then this hunter-doctor is expected too?

ANN. Sartin! Rachel wouldn't take no for an answer. She said she was afeared to travel without her physician, an' the Captain swears in good sound cuss words that his nuss shall make his hum here for a year at least!

DYKE. Rachel writes in glowing terms of her new friend, then?

ANN. Glowin'? Well—she jist glows all over—she says he's the tallest, strongest, handsomest, self-sacrificin'st man she ever see. Ahem!

DYKE. I trust a further acquaintance will give her no cause to change her sentiments, I'm sure. And as any service rendered her is fully appreciated by me, I shall avail myself of an early opportunity to thank this handsome stranger for his care and attention to my fair cousin.

ANN. Yes—I'd so advise, as your fair cousin looks to see Mr. Wynthrop well received by all who call themselves her friends!

DYKE. [*Bows as if to satisfy her of his sincere intentions*] And now—tell me, Mrs. Campbell, how do you like active service?

ANN. What d'ye mean by active service? [*Stops churning*]

DYKE. Is not Sir Frederick Shelton quartered here?

ANN. Oh! Yes, ef that's what you mean—but I want yeou to understand that I hain't in his active service, nor in the active service of any Britisher that ever wore scarlet.

DYKE. Captain Winslow and he were brother officers in the Old French War, I believe?

ANN. Yes. An' when the Captain heard of Sir Frederick's rigimint bein' camped near here, he writ to hev Sir Frederick an' his staff make themselves to hum in this house till he returned. They've done so—an' while I've too much respect for the old Captain to disrespect any guest o' his'n, when it comes to active service, you'll find me on the other side o' the fence tooth an' nail. America's my country! An' if it comes to a fight, I can carry a musket an' use it too as well as the next man. Active service indeed! [*Takes butter out of churn and slaps it into wooden bowl with a bang. Characteristic music to take Dyke off and bring Reuben*[1] *and Roanoke on*]

DYKE. Dear Mrs. Campbell, neither your courage nor your skill are to be doubted! I thank you for your cheerfully given information and will endeavor to be present at the reception of our expected guests. Good-day to you!

ANN. Good-day—an' don't forgit that I'm allus ready for active service, but it must be in a righteous cause! [*Takes butter and exits through rear of dairy*]

DYKE. [*Turning to go R.1.E.*] So! So! a new found friend who may prove a rival! This must be looked to. I must press the Captain to a speedy fulfillment of his promise. Delays are dangerous—to lose the girl were to lose all! All? No—should I not still hold her fortune? Fortune? Jove! Dyke

[1] In the manuscript this character's name is spelt "Rueben," evidently through an error of the copyist.

Hampton, would you deceive yourself? The fortune of a monarch would not content you without her. Your passionate love for her burns in your veins and swells your heart till you pant and thirst like the tracking bloodhound, and, like him, you will not be balked of your prey. Faugh! It may be but a scare after all. Forewarned is forearmed—and I start with the advantage on my side! [*Exit slowly R.1.E. Music increases and Reuben enters followed by Roanoke, U.E.R. Reuben quaintly dressed in hunting costume but carries no gun. A man of 55 years or thereabouts. Iron gray hair which he wears long, no beard—face weatherbeaten and grizzled, but bearing the stamp of perpetual good-nature and generosity. He carries a bundle of herbs. Roanoke, a tall, handsome young Indian, of 25 years or so, face as light as a man heavily tanned and sunburned. He must be straight as an arrow and lithe as a willow. He is fully and picturesquely costumed (see plate), carries a rifle and game, consisting of squirrels, pigeons and small birds. Music drops as they begin dialogue and finally dies away*]

REU. Roanoke, you've begun the week well, as the feller said who was to be hanged on a Monday. Pigeons, plover, squirrels! You're airly on the wing, as the worm said to the robin! [*Reuben L., Roanoke R.*]

ROAN. Roanoke is never lighter of heart, fleeter of limb, stronger of arm or surer of aim, than when serving a friend. He would fret like a wounded deer could he not bring his share of the feast that is to welcome home the White Captain and his beautiful daughter!

REU. Right you are. It's more blessed to give than to receive, as the mate said when he flogged the cabin boy—an' you're allus a'givin' an' a'doin' suthin' for the Captain, Rachel or my Dorothy!

ROAN. Dorothy—the Little Primrose—voice like the matin' song of the lark—laugh like the rippling water—eyes like the liquid dew-drop—step like the bounding fawn—shedding life and joy on every living thing blessed by the sunlight of her presence! Roanoke like all else loves her. The Great Spirit watch over and protect her—and the vengeance of Roanoke on him who wounds her even by a look!

REU. That's Injun all over, that is. Let an Injun love anything an' he's—all—Injun. Let him hate anything an' he's—well—he's all Injun too! [*Music pp. till Roanoke off*]

ROAN. Why should not the Indian love the sweet Primrose? Has she not taught him all he knows beyond the ways of his tribe? Has she not brought light to his darkened mind—taught him to read the grand books—told him tales of the brave warriors and mighty hunters, who have gone before—taught him to shrink from the cruelties of his race—to love only that that is good and beautiful—to hope that he might one day be something more than a mere Indian—and be worthy to pluck the pretty Primrose, plant it in his heart, there to blossom and bloom forever?

REU. Roanoke—there's a good deal o' man in yeou—as Jonah said to the whale's belly—an' when that little Primrose makes up her mind just where she wants to be transplanted, I ain't a'goin' to say a word agin' her choice, so long's the soil's fresh 'n sweet 'a kep well watered by truth, honesty 'n manhood. I can't expect to keep her allus. When the time comes I'll give her up—with an achin' heart meb'be, but I'll give her up all the same. An' now let's find Mrs. Campbell an' hand over our plunder. That's a great woman, Roanoke—Mrs. Campbell is—she ain't no primrose an' they ain't much boundin' fawn left in her, but fur fryin' doughnuts, darnin' a feller's stockin's, nussin' a sick baby, or smoothin' a dyin' woman's piller—I'll put her agin' any woman in Massachusetts!

ROAN. Give her these, Father Reuben. [*Gives game*] Say Roanoke sends them with his best love, and will return to greet the White Captain and bid him welcome home!

REU. [*Taking game*] Be sure yeou do git back. Yeour face'd be one o' the fust to be missed by the Captain ye know.

ROAN. Roanoke will return—fear not! [*Exit through trees at back, looking around house and at windows in hope of getting a glimpse of Dorothy. At same time enter from house C., Ann Campbell. Music ceases. Reuben turns from looking after Roanoke and meets her*]

REU. Ah! Mrs. Campbell!

ANN. Hello! Reuben! That yeou?

REU. Yes. I was jist goin' to look you up. Me'n Roanoke's been a'huntin'. I dunno's Roanoke's hunted any more'n I hev, but he found more—them's his'n. [*Gives game*] An' them's mine! [*Gives herbs*]

ANN. [*Smelling them*] Sassafras! How good it does smell! Thank ye—I was afeared you'd forgit it!

REU. Forgitten ain't one o' my strong points—but—say—Ann—er, Mrs. Campbell—what on airth be ye agoin' to do with all them 'ere yarbs?

ANN. Experimint—don't intend to drink no chiny tea till the tax's took off. Mean to try fust one thing an' then another an' sometime I'll hit on suthin'll make as good tea if not better'n chiny tea. This is a great country an' everything ain't found out yit. There's checkerberry now—it makes good tea 'f tain't allowed to bile. Bile checkerberry an' it loses its vartue.

REU. I've e'en a'most forgot the taste o' chiny tea myself. I ain't drinked no checkerberry—but I've swallered enough Balm o' Gillead—sage—mountain mint—sweet fern an' catnip to start a pothecary in bizzness.

ANN. I love 'em—every one on 'em! There's a flavor of freedom in 'em all!

REU. Freedom's all very well, but what's the use o' lyin' when the truth kin be proved agin' ye—an' I say I'd give a good deal for a cup o' good ole-fashioned chiny tea, all the same!

ANN. Well—ef yeou wait for Ann Campbell to brew it for ye—ye'll hev checkerberry a sproutin' out all over ye, an' catnip juice a'oozin' out'n yer finer e'ends! What's the news over in Boston?

REU. There was a big meetin' in ole Tunnel last night. Sam Adams an' Dr. Warren made some purty strong speechifyin'—they say there's no way out'n it 'cept fight!

ANN. Fight! That's it! Fight! That's the way out'n it—an' the sooner it comes the better say I!

REU. It'll make purty hard times! [*Looking at her slyly*]

ANN. Hard times ain't a'goin' to skeer me, nor hard blows—nuthin' if it comes to that!

REU. Talkin' o' fightin', what's come o' Dorothy? [*Dorothy's music begins pp., swells as she enters and dies away during her scene*]

ANN. Cleanin' house! She wouldn't let me lay a finger on a blessed thing in Rachel's room. She's been as busy as a bee all day, and she hed that English *Imitation* soldier a'runnin' around like mad—luggin' water an' a'sweepin' an' a'dustin', an' the sweat a'runnin' off'n him like rain off from a duck's back. The last I see on 'em, she hed an apron on him an' he was a settin' on the winder lidge, cleanin' winders!

REU. Well, she couldn't put the British Army to better use, I'm sure! [*Dorothy laughs in house*] Hello—talk o' the ole boy—

DOR. [*In house*] What, an officer, and can't pare apples! Where's your military education?

SMOL. [*In house*] Dear Miss Foxglove, paring apples does not come under the head of military tactics!

DOR. [*In house*] Oh! Nonsense! Soldiers should know everything! [*Laughs*]

REU. It seems to be gineral trainin' day with her. I'll make myself scurse or she'll want to press me into the service! [*Exit U.E.R. laughing and looking back at house. At same time Ann exits with game and herbs, through dairy. Music swells with Dorothy's laughter till it becomes a perfect burst as she enters and then quiets down and gradually dies away. She has knife and wooden bowl; dressed handsomely and has large apron over all; locket on slender chain around neck. She is immediately followed by Smollet, who has coat sleeves rolled up, English Lieutenant's Undress Uniform, a woman's apron on and carries a pan of apples. Smollet is an elegant English gentleman, full of humor, and gallantry. Dorothy, the quintessence of roguish and witching comedy. Smollet protests and she will not listen till they are well on the stage*]

DOR. [*Laughing*] There! There! Don't talk! Let us get to work! Or there will be no pie for supper. I declare you've done nothing but talk this blessed day!

SMOL. [*R. protesting good-naturedly*] But dear Miss Foxglove, suppose Sir Frederick were to surprise me?

DOR. He will never surprise you in better company, nor in a more useful occupation!

SMOL. Do let us retire to the kitchen, the proper place for—

DOR. The kitchen is too hot! *I'm* hot!

SMOL. Warm!

DOR. No! Hot! When I'm warm, I'm warm; and when I'm hot, I'm hot. And now I'm *hot!* [*Looking at him decidedly*]

SMOL. Yes! Hot! [*Eyeing her with a smile. She bows as if satisfied*] The rear porch, then!

DOR. Lieutenant Smollet—

SMOL. [*Correcting her*] *Smollet,* please!

DOR. Smullet!

SMOL. Smollet!

DOR. Smallet!

SMOL. Smollet! S-m-o-l-l-e-t—permit me to know my own name, please!

DOR. Smollet! Excuse me—I—you are ashamed to be found in my company and engaged in the useful occupation of paring apples. Why—[*Attempts to take apples from him*]

SMOL. Oh! Good gracious—no! Only too happy to be near you under any circumstances—I assure you!

DOR. Then sit down and let us get to work: [*Seats him on steps of porch. Sits near him. Business of arranging the apples and getting closer and closer to him until she is quite snug and comfortable. Looks at him archly during all this. He plays this entire scene with extreme good nature, but is at no time the slightest particle silly. She now begins to pare apples. Finds knife dull and after one or two attempts stops*] Oh! Pshaw! What a knife! It's as dull as a hoe! It wouldn't cut butter if it were hot! I'll run and get another! [*Attempts to rise*]

SMOL. [*Preventing*] Oh! No! No! No! Don't do that—here, take my penknife! [*Offering it*]

DOR. That will never do, Lieutenant! They say that to give a person a knife is a sure sign of a quarrel! [*Archly*]

SMOL. But I don't intend to give it—only lend it to you!

DOR. Oh! [*Simply*] That's a different thing altogether. Thank you. [*Takes his knife; gives him hers*] You can use this—strop it a little on your belt. [*Both begin work*] Now we are all right. You can talk. We'll both work. Be sure you say pretty things to me. [*Laughs*] And I'll keep a look out for my boy. He generally needs his mother about this time, so he's sure to be along presently to hunt me up!

SMOL. Boy! Good gracious! Miss Foxglove, do you mean to say that you are a mother?

DOR. [*Without looking up*] Umps.

SMOL. Where's your husband?

DOR. Never had one!

SMOL. Miss Foxglove!

DOR. Fact, I assure you!

SMOL. And you are a mother?

DOR. Yes!

SMOL. How long have you been a mother?

DOR. Ever since I can remember!

SMOL. Good gracious! How old is your boy, pray?

DOR. About fifty.

SMOL. Most extraordinary! May I ask how you call him?

DOR. Whistle for him! Or blow the horn!

SMOL. [*Laughing*] No! No! What's his name?

DOR. Reuben Foxglove!

SMOL. [*Laughs heartily*] Oh! I see! And *you* are *his* mother?

DOR. The only one he has—and a precious trouble he is too, I can tell you—always losing his buttons!

SMOL. You Colonists!

DOR. Americans, please!

SMOL. Beg pardon. Americans are singular people!

DOR. Strange! That's exactly what we think of you English!

SMOL. I dare say, but I have failed to find in England the case of a daughter being mother to her own father!

DOR. Quite a common thing in America!

SMOL. Really?

DOR. Really!

SMOL. Humph! Miss Foxglove, I'm an orphan!

DOR. You look it!

SMOL. Do I really?

DOR. You do, really!

SMOL. Would you mind twins?

DOR. Lieutenant!

SMOL. [*Quickly*] No! No! No! I don't mean that that—but would you mind being a mother to me? I never thought of it before but now that you've put it into my head I believe I need a mother!

DOR. I believe you do!

SMOL. I'm *sure* I do. And then think what a large circle of relatives we should have and all within ourselves, as I may say! You would be your husband's mother and I'd be my wife's son and my father-in-law's father and he'd be his son-in-law's son and father-in-law's son's mother—sisters—e—e—at all events we should be quite a snug family party, don't you think so?

DOR. And when you were naughty boys, I could punish you both and put you to bed, eh?

SMOL. That would be charming, I'm sure!

DOR. But Lieutenant! Won't it be rather awkward when this war breaks out, to have my two children fight against each other?

SMOL. Dear Miss Foxglove, there will be no war!

DOR. What makes you think so?

SMOL. The Colonists.

DOR. Americans! [*Looking at him correctingly*]

SMOL. Americans [*Bowing*] will never think of resisting when the powerful armies of England are sent against them. It would be a useless slaughter of brave men. Your leaders will think better of it. Fight? What for?

DOR. Liberty! The grandest word ever uttered by the tongue of man! I tell you, Lieutenant, you have to fight for everything you get in this world. We Colonists, as you call us, have fought the savages for our land, the land inch by inch for our crops—the hungry wolves and prowling bears for our bleating sheep and their innocent lambs—and now we'll fight the King's soldiers for that most priceless of God's gifts—Liberty—and think it cheaply purchased by the best blood of our country!

SMOL. [*Amazed*] Good gracious, Miss Foxglove, I had no intention of wounding your feelings. I assure you I am extremely sorry. I was wrong to—

DOR. And I, Lieutenant—pardon *me*. I should not allow my feelings to carry me away. I am thoroughly American—that must be my excuse for this breach of politeness, to say the least. You are an Englishman and our guest. [*He bows. She changes her manner and breaks into a laugh*] But it's all the fault of that jackknife! Take it back. I never wish to see it again. [*He takes it*] Am I forgiven?

SMOL. Freely! Dear Miss Foxglove!

DOR. And now let us dismiss a subject that never should have been broached between us!

SMOL. With all my heart! What an unique medallion that is you have! [*Points to locket*] English, is it not?

DOR. [*Hastily, covering it with both hands and rising*] I do not know. It was, I believe, my mother's. In it is all I have ever known of her. I prize it so dearly, that I seldom wear it. [*The chain has broken as she clutched it and comes off her neck*]

SMOL. There! You've broken the chain—all my fault—how stupid of me!

DOR. Oh! that's nothing. The chain is very slight. I'll put it on a ribbon presently! [*Puts it in pocket*] Speaking of ribbons, reminds me that I have not decorated you yet!

SMOL. Oh! I am to be decorated? What for, pray?

DOR. Gallant conduct in the field! [*Pinning apple paring on his left breast*] That's for polishing the silver. [*Puts one on right breast*] That's for cleaning the windows so nicely!

SMOL. You are too good! [*Dubiously*]

DOR. [*Putting one on left ear*] That's for being the *dear, good-natured, courteous gentleman that you are.*

SMOL. [*Pleased*] Thank you!

DOR. [*Putting one on right ear*] And this, wear as the colors of your lady, whose beauty you are to defend against all comers!

SMOL. Believe me, I will prize the last beyond all else in life!

DOR. There! Now stand up! [*He does so*] And let me see how you look on dress parade! [*He has the pan of apples. She puts him in position*] Attention! Heads up! [*Reuben comes on at back*] Forward—march! [*They march down stairs*] File left! [*They do so*] File left! [*They do so*]

REU. [*At back*] Halt! [*They stop suddenly and all laugh*] Dorothy, you was a filin' left with the wrong foot!

SMOL. I dare say I look quite ridiculous, Mr. Foxglove!

REU. Yes, quite—but I've been there myself!

DOR. Reuben Foxglove, don't you interfere with my army! We are just going to make the pies, aren't we, Lieutenant?

SMOL. Yes, certainly, anything to oblige!

DOR. And the Lieutenant is going to help me with the crust. So please don't bother us now. [*About to go, looks at Reuben, sees button off his coat*] Oh! Good gracious! Oh! Dear me! [*Thrusts her bowl hastily into Smollet's pan*] Hold that! [*Runs to Reuben*] Now, Reuben Foxglove, where's that button? [*Talks breathlessly, shaking her head at him. At same time takes threaded needle and thimble from quaint bag at her side*] Oh! Dear! Dear! What a boy you are for losing buttons! When you left home this morning, every button was in its place, and you come to me now with the most prominent one gone, for gone I'm sure it is. You're never on speaking terms with any of them. They leave you—

REU. [*Who has quietly taken button from pocket*] On the slightest provocation. Only this one [*Handing it*] I managed to ketch jest as he was a'sneakin' off the last thread!

DOR. Give it to me, stupid boy! [*Dorothy's music pp. till Sir Frederick on and off, then change to lively to bring Winslow's party on*] Sit down. [*Seats him on old plow. Kneels in front of him and sews button playing scene over shoulder at Lieutenant*] Tired, Lieutenant?

SMOL. Not at all. Quite a recreation, I assure you.

REU. Say, Dorothy, hain't yeou an' him rather chummy for a rebel and a Britisher?

DOR. He's perfectly harmless, aren't you, Lieutenant?

SMOL. [*Who has not heard what she said*] Yes! Yes! Certainly! [*All laugh. Sir Frederick Shelton, a fine-looking, middle-aged English gentleman, very elegant, very dignified, in undress of Colonel of Grenadiers, strolls on quietly; stops; views the position of the parties in some amazement. By this time Dorothy has finished button and rises*]

DOR. [*Putting things in bag*] There you are—all right—and tight, once more! Now, Lieutenant—[*Going towards him, sees Sir Frederick. Stops and curtseys very low*] Sir Frederick, your most obedient! [*Sir Frederick acknowledges salute*]

SMOL. Sir Frederick—who—what? [*Turns and sees him*] The Devil! I beg pardon, sir. The fact is—I—she—you—[*Confusedly endeavoring to salute, etc.*]

DOR. There, there! Don't stammer. [*Goes to him, rights the bowl and pan*] The fact is, Sir Frederick, I've enlisted him in the domestic brigade till roll call, when I'll return him to you right side up with care. Attention! [*Slips arm through Smollet's arm*] Forward! [*Marches him into house and off L.H. laughing heartily, in which Reuben joins. Sir Frederick follows, looking after them good-naturedly, then comes down C.*]

SIR F. [*To Reuben, who has dropped down R. After a pause, slowly*] Your daughter?

REU. [*Looking at him suspiciously*] Ye-e-s!

SIR F. May I ask her age?

REU. [*Same manner*] Nineteen!

SIR F. Her mother—

REU. Died when she was a baby.

SIR F. And you have brought her up?

REU. [*As before*] Ye-e-s!

SIR F. She has attended school? [*Smollet with dress arranged enters and remains respectfully at back*]

REU. Ye-e-s—somewhat.

SIR F. She seems a charming girl!

REU. She *is!*

SIR F. She must be a blessing to you!

REU. She is!

SIR F. A very charming girl!

REU. Ye-e-s! [*Sir Frederick bows very proudly and goes down stage. Reuben bows politely and strolls off at back R., looking at Sir Frederick as if some dread haunted him. Smollet drops down L. of Sir Frederick*]

SIR F. Strange how that girl affects me. Her age—her likeness to—Pshaw! Impossible! Poor wronged Agnes—[*Sadly, then changing to half anger*] why will that woman always haunt me? She must be—she *is* dead—both dead—no trace of either for nearly twenty years. [*Sadly*] Dead! But does her death atone for the wrong I did her? Alas! No! That can never *be* atoned.

SMOL. Miss Foxglove always seems to affect you strangely, Sir Frederick.

SIR F. [*Starting, as if from a reverie*] Yes! In my daily intercourse with her, I seem to live the past over again; to catch a glimpse of that Heaven which might have been mine, had I not wantonly closed my doors against an angel's love!

DOR. [*From house, running on backwards, speaking as she enters. Runs against Sir Frederick and Smollet, and off at back R.H. Jumping and clapping hands with glee*] Here they come! Here they come! Mrs. Campbell! Father! Where are you? I'm so happy I can't contain myself! They're coming, I tell you! I must be the first to meet them! Rachel! Rachel! Don't speak to anyone till I've kissed you. [*Runs off*]

ANN. [*Who has hurried on through dairy*] Mercy on us! That gal's enough to give one the hystericks!

SIR F. Who is coming, may I ask?

ANN. The Captain and Rachel, I suppose, by the way *she* goes on! [*Goes up; looks off R.*] Yes, there they be, sure as a gun!

SIR F. [*To Smollet*] I shall be glad to shake the hand of my old comrade and thank him for his hospitality. Let us retire for the present, however, lest we mar the welcome these good people have prepared. [*They exeunt*

R.1E. Music changes to lively air. Enter from R. at back, Captain Winslow, leaning on the arm of Roanoke, the Captain a dark, little old man, with white military whiskers; semi-military in dress and wholly so in manner; lame in right leg; carries a cane. Ann Campbell wipes old-fashioned chair and places it R.C. for him. Rachel and Dorothy come, arms around each other's waists, drop L.C. Reuben and Ned follow—Ned in handsome hunting costume. They join ladies. The entrance all animation. All talk together till Captain is seated and stage dressed]

CAPT. [*As he enters*] Thank ye. Thank ye. I'm as glad to get home as you are to see me, I'm sure!

ANN. [*As they enter*] Well, well, sakes alive, if they ain't jest as nat'ral as life!

DOR. [*As she enters*] Oh, Rachel, I'm so happy! I've got so much to tell you!

RACH. [*As she enters*] Dear old Dorothy, it seems as if I had not seen you for an age!

REU. [*As he enters*] Well, I hope you'll make yourself to hum. No ceremony wanted here!

NED. [*As he enters*] Thank you! Thank you! I'm sure!

CAPT. What a demonstration to be sure! One would think we had returned from a trip to the Antipodes! Well, I must say it is pleasant to be welcome even in one's own home. [*Taking chair and Ann's hand*] Mrs. Campbell, I hope Reuben has been civil to you during my absence!

ANN. Civil! I'd like to catch him bein' anything else to me! Captain, the sight on ye is good for sore eyes! [*Goes to place and is introduced to Ned. Curtseys*]

CAPT. Reuben, old friend, how go things with you?

REU. I jog along about the same old sixpence, Captain, sometimes walking on the balance on foot!

CAPT. And Roanoke! My faithful Roanoke! I've missed you sadly, boy—I don't know why—only that I love to look on your bright, manly face—and the day seemed to lack something without it. I hope Dorothy has been behaving herself. Here, Dorothy, you mischievous puss, come and give me another kiss. [*She does so*] I hope you have not been breaking poor Roanoke's heart!

DOR. Roanoke knows me too well to mind my idle pranks. [*Crosses to Roanoke and, giving him her hand, seriously*] I could not wound the thing I love—and I love—[*Checking herself*]—we *all* love Roanoke!

ROAN. White Captain, the little Primrose grows in the path of Roanoke. Its scent fills the air of his life. He is happy. [*He has taken her right hand in his right, placed his left arm around her waist and almost drawn her to his breast. She yields, then suddenly but not urgently checks the impulse*]

Dor. Isn't Mr. Wynthrop handsome? [*Military music behind scenes, distant, kept up till cue to cease. Roanoke looks into her face for a moment, drops her hand, she crosses to her former position. At same instant an orderly enters from R.1E. and salutes*]

Orderly. Captain Winslow?

Capt. [*Saluting*] I have that honor. [*Orderly marches up to him, salutes, gives paper, faces about. Marches back to place, faces about, awaits orders. Captain reads written letter*] "Sir Frederick Shelton presents his compliments to Captain Winslow and politely requests him, if not too fatigued, to witness regimental drill of His Majesty's Grenadiers, after which Sir Frederick will do himself the honor of dining with his old comrade and friend." [*To Orderly*] I shall attend Sir Frederick's pleasure—say so. [*Orderly salutes, faces and marches off*] Reuben and Roanoke, I shall need your assistance. This infernal fighting leg of mine, you know! Mr. Wynthrop, will you accompany us?

Ned. Thank you, Captain! No! His Majesty's soldiers have no charm for me at present, though they may have later on!

Capt. Ah, Rebel, take care! I leave Rachel and Dorothy to entertain you till I return. [*Bows and exits, E.R. leaning on Roanoke and accompanied by Reuben*]

Ann. Ef you'll excuse me, I'll give the finishin' touches to the table. [*Exit through dairy*]

Dor. And my pies forgotten in the oven. I'll bet a cookie they're burnt to a cinder. [*Goes up to door, then down to Rachel. Aside*] He's handsomer than Mr. Hampton. I *love* a handsome man. You go right ahead. If anyone comes, I'll cough. Ahem! See? [*By-play between her and Rachel. She chuckles and exits into house and off L.*]

Ned. This is indeed a charming spot, Miss Winslow. [*He offers arm. She takes it. They stroll and finally Rachel seats herself on rustic seat L.H.*] I can now understand your glowing eulogisms on your Massachusetts home. Were you born here, may I ask?

Rach. Yes—beneath that roof my brother Harry and I entered and our dear mother left, this world. I have known and wish to know no other home.

Ned. Your brother was your elder, I believe?

Rach. Three years.

Ned. He suddenly and mysteriously disappeared, your father told me.

RACH. Yes. My father was absent with his regiment at the time, my mother an invalid, and I a baby by her side.

NED. Was his fate never learned?

RACH. Oh, yes! Mr. Hampton, who made the most strenuous exertions in our behalf, brought incontestable proofs that he had been stolen and murdered by a band of Mohawk Indians who committed many depredations in this vicinity about that time. My poor mother never spoke after the news was broken to her. She passed silently away, I hope, to join the boy she loved so dearly.

NED. Mr. Hampton! Humph! It is he, I think your father also told me, who by your uncle's will inherits the estate which should have been your brother's had he lived.

RACH. Yes. He is my father's cousin.

NED. And a claimant for your hand?

RACH. [*Hanging her head*] He has asked my *father* for my hand.

NED. And you?

RACH. Have promised to marry him.

NED. May I ask if you love him?

RACH. [*Rising*] Mr. Wynthrop!

NED. Pardon. Did it never occur to you that Mr. Hampton might be interested in your brother's death?

RACH. You go too far, sir.

NED. Again your pardon. Stranger things have been known.

RACH. I must not listen to you, sir!

NED. I crave one moment. I have thought that were there a way out of this marriage you would avail yourself of it. Is it so?

RACH. By what right do you ask?

NED. The right an honest man has to undo a wrong. Listen to a little romance. [*Seats her*] Once upon a time there lived two children, a boy and a girl, both motherless, who, thrown much together, learned to love each other as only children can, and in the impulses of their fresh young hearts plighted their youthful troths, vowing that nothing but death should separate them—that if they lived they should become man and wife. The boy's father died, and cruel fate bound him to a crueller master in the form of one Dyke Hampton. One outrage succeeded another, until at last, stung beyond endurance, the boy dared to resent an infamous wrong and was, for his bravery, felled to the earth by a blow from his brutal master. Crushed, bleeding, but not subdued, the boy crept silently away into the shadows of the night and was seen no more, but before he went he sent a message to his baby bride telling her that if he lived he would sure return.

RACH. [*Who has slowly risen, having drunk in every word he uttered, with a wild cry*] Man! Man! Who are you?

NED. Ned Farnsworth. [*She shrieks and falls into his arms*] Your boy lover! [*Military music ceases*]

RACH. Ned! My Ned!

DOR. [*Entering hurriedly from house*] What's the matter? Doctor pulling your tooth? [*Takes in the situation*] Excuse me—my pies are burning! [*Exit hurriedly into house again*]

RACH. Ned, why did you not tell?

NED. Because the time had not come. Nor must I now be known by any here save as Mr. Wynthrop, your accidental friend. But Rachel, the day is far distant when Dyke Hampton calls wife the woman who pledged her baby troth to Ned Farnsworth. [*Enter Sergeant and file of Soldiers. When they are in position*]

SERG. Halt! [*They do so*] Front! [*They do so*] Present! [*Enter Sir Frederick in full dress and Winslow, arm in arm, followed by Smollet in full dress, Reuben and Roanake as they pass on*] Recover! [*They do so*] Right face! [*They do so*] Forward, by file right, march! [*Men march off*]

CAPT. Wynthrop, you missed a grand sight! It does an old soldier's heart good to witness such discipline and precision. Rachel, girl, welcome my old friend, Sir Frederick Shelton. My daughter, Sir Frederick. [*They bow. Dorothy's music till end of act, very piano at first, works with scene*]

RACH. [*Crossing, taking Sir Frederick's hand*] Proud to meet any friend of my father's, sir.

CAPT. [*Introducing*] Mr. Wynthrop, my Galen of the forest. [*They bow*] Daughter, Lieutenant Smollet. [*They bow*] Mr. Wynthrop. [*Smollet and Ned bow*] Rachel, give your arm to Sir Frederick. The Lieutenant will follow. Wynthrop and myself will bring up the rear—and so far—

DOR. [*Appearing on steps, locket on neck on ribbon*] Supper! [*All laugh. Rachel gives arm to Sir Frederick. Ned passes over to Winslow. Smollet crosses up behind Winslow. General movement. As Sir Frederick goes up he keeps his eyes on Dorothy. As he nears her he sees locket, stands transfixed, then slowly retreats with back to audience—seems to half faint. Smollet rushes to him, placing chair. He sinks into it. Ned goes to Rachel. All advance*]

SIR F. [*Recovering himself, speaking slowly and in hoarse whisper*] In God's name, girl—how came you by that locket?

DOR. It was clasped around my neck when Reuben found me—placed there, as I believe and hope, by my mother before she died.

SIR F. [*Same tone*] Why have I not seen it before?

DOR. I never wear it but on holidays and Sundays. It is too sacred for every day. [*Half frightened by his manner*] Why do you look at me so strangely? You frighten me! Reuben! Roanoke! [*Roanoke springs down R. She crosses quickly to him and shelters herself in his arms. Reuben drops down also*]

SIR F. Found—Reuben—found. Are you not then his child?

REU. In all that makes her so cept'n blood—an' that's better done a'thout sometimes.

SIR F. If not your child, whose is she?

REU. God's, I reckon. Leastwise, he give her to me!

SIR F. [*In whisper as before*] Her story!

REU. One terrible snowy night, eighteen years ago, after buildin' a big fire on my hearth, I went as usual to bait and set my traps. When I got back I found my cabin door open—the wind, I reckon, had undid the latch. I entered an' right on the hearth afore the fire I see suthin' a'shinin' bright an' yaller—jest like gold. I stooped to pick it up, an' it was hair—bright, golden, shiny hair—an' there was this child—this angel baby—a'lyin' on my cabin floor an' sleepin' as gently an' as peacefully as if she was a nussin' from her mother's breast.

SIR F. [*Almost overcome with grief and excitement, as before*] Go on!

REU. I will. [*Wipes eyes*] At fust I kinder conjured as how some one must a'left her there, an' I stepped to the door to look around. It had stopped snowin' an' the moon was a'shinin' bright as day—not a sound 'cept the howlin' o' the wolves. I was about to close the door agin when I see the baby's footsteps in the snow. I follered 'em, an' a thin ten paces came on the form of a woman lyin' in the snow. She was dead. Then I see it all. The woman had got lost in the storm. She tried to reach my cabin—fell exhausted—the child must a' rolled from her arms an', baby like, attracted by the light, toddled to my door. Heaven opened it for her—she crept in—the warm fire lulled her to sleep—an' there I found her! [*During this scene, Dorothy has crept to him, sobbing and almost buried herself in his bosom*]

SIR F. [*As before*] And that locket was clasped around her neck?

REU. Yes!

SIR F. Have you ever opened it?

REU. Tried to, but couldn't. Allus thought there wan't no openin' to it.

SIR F. Let me see it!

DOR. [*Clasping it with both hands*] No—no—you shall not!

SIR F. [*Gently*] Fear nothing, child. I will restore it.

REU. [*Half afraid*] Let him see it, Dorothy. No harm can come to it. [*He gently unties it from her neck and passes it to Sir Frederick, who rolls it over in his hand and it opens*]

SIR F. [*Springing up with a wild scream*] See! My marriage certificate! Her mother's likeness! She is my child!

ALL. Your child!

DOR. [*Screams and clings to Reuben*] No! No! Don't listen, Reuben! He's mad! *Here* is my father! You'll break his heart—you'll kill me. Give me back my locket. Shut it up! [*Springs towards Sir Frederick*] Reuben! Roanoke! Don't let him take me! I—Oh! Ha—ha—ha! [*Screams—laughs hysterically and falls in Reuben's arms as curtain descends*]

PICTURE AND END OF ACT I.

ACT II.

(*"Descriptive music" to take up curtain*)

TIME: *April 1775.*

SCENE 1: *Dorchester Heights. Interior of old-fashioned kitchen, roofed; with large old-fashioned fireplace, crane, log fire, etc. Heavy beams or rafters on which are hung dried apples, tufts of herbs, bunches of onions, crook-neck squash, bell peppers, etc. Everything about this scene—furniture, pots, pans, dishes, etc., must be historically correct. Same backing as Act I. At Rise: Evening. Scene lighted wholly by fire-log. Towards end of Act it grows dark outside and moon rises. Ann Campbell discovered washing dishes in (smoking) hot water. She pays no attention to scene. After she has finished the dishes she carries them off R. door. Returns, wipes up table, takes dish-pan, etc. and exits R.D. Returns after a bit with lighted candle and exits up the stairs as if to go to bed. Rachel is spinning. Captain Winslow smoking pipe. He is very careworn and smokes slowly and thoughtfully. Dyke Hampton is seated cross-legged on chair with its back in front of him—he is dressed as before—with addition of top coat. He is in the act of receiving papers from Captain Winslow.*

DYKE. I am glad the accounts are correct. My father, during his life, left undone nothing that in his judgment would enhance your interests; and I as his successor, have, I trust, been fully as vigilant. Yet, in spite of all, we have not succeeded so well as we could have wished.

CAPT. You have succeeded in leaving me a beggar!

DYKE. Captain—I—

CAPT. You say the Van Orten suit has been decided against me?

DYKE. [*Slowly, as if loathe to admit it*] Y-e-s!

CAPT. And that tomorrow he will claim this, my last bit of property?

DYKE. Unless certain conditions can be met!

CAPT. Which you know I cannot meet!

DYKE. Not without assistance—I am aware.

CAPT. Dyke—I don't say that my property has been wrongfully managed. It is too late for that now. But it is singular that while I have grown steadily poor, you have grown *as* steadily rich.

DYKE. Do you blame me for having prospered?

CAPT. I blame no one—I say it's strange, that's all.

DYKE. You forget that my cousin, your brother, added materially to my worldly store!

CAPT. Poor Edward—basely deceived by the only woman he ever loved, he could not forgive my daughter's birth. Had he ever looked into her face, he had not been so cruel in his will.

DYKE. I will not say that he was altogether just. The fact remains nevertheless—that—your son dead—the property comes to me. I, therefore, should be wrong to quarrel with the memory of the giver. I can, however, correct his error. Let this marriage between Rachel and myself take place at once and half your brother's estate is yours. [*Weird pathetic music now till Dyke off and Reuben on*]

CAPT. You ask me to sell my own flesh and blood?

DYKE. No! Your word and hers are both pledged to the union—and—[*Humbly*] am I not worthy of her? [*With passionate intensity*] I tell you I love your daughter with a passion beyond the conception of other men—I would for her sake—

RACH. [*Looking up, smiling sadly, with cheek on hand, leaning on the knee of her father*] Be generous?

DYKE. [*As if avoiding a trap*] *How*—generous?

RACH. Give—me—up! [*Same tone*]

DYKE. Do—you—love another? [*Slowly, passionately, almost between his teeth*]

RACH. [*Droops head and says quietly*] We are never masters of our own hearts!

DYKE. [*Springing up with violent passion—overturning chair and raising aloft clenched hand in which he holds whip*] Then—by God—I'll kill him! [*Rachel, who has sprung up and clung about her father's neck, utters a smothered scream and hides her face*]

CAPT. [*Who has risen at same time, says sternly and with his old dignity and fire*] Hampton—you forget yourself!

DYKE. [*Recovering and trembling with excitement*] Yes—I—my feelings —forgive me—I'll leave you—a gallop across the hills will compose me. [*Crosses to L.H. door*] I'm unstrung. [*Turns and speaks moodily*] Rachel—you are a woman and I ask you to pity me from a woman's heart. For something tells me that my love for you is the chain that will yet drag me down to infamy and eternal damnation. Don't judge me wrongfully. I value wealth only as it serves to bind you to me—with you—I might be—[*Almost tempted to betray all he knows, then checks himself*] I cannot say—without you, I *know* I shall be a *Devil*. You ask me to give you up. Well, what then, to another? [*Through teeth*] No! Never! [*Change*] That is—I'm afraid I could not. [*With moody ferocity*] Don't tempt me. I tremble for you. I tremble for him, I tremble for myself. I'll go now—pardon me. [*Gets near door, then turns*] I love you, Rachel. [*Looks earnestly at her*] Good-night. [*Exit. Rachel pale and calm on her father's breast. He looking after Dyke. Picture. Pause*]

RACH. [*Coldly*] Father—I'll marry Dyke.

CAPT. Do you love him?

RACH. No! But I fear him—I must save him—I must save you—I must save—

CAPT. [*Reading her thoughts*] Wynthrop?

RACH. [*Same tone*] Yes.

CAPT. You love Wynthrop?

RACH. Else I'd never marry Hampton!

CAPT. Will Wynthrop consent to this?

RACH. He must—he will. He loves me!

CAPT. [*Bitterly*] And yet he deserts you! Disappears in the dead of night, leaving no word, no token, and is as utterly lost to you as if the earth had opened and swallowed him!

RACH. He will return—and if not—it were better so.

CAPT. My poor child—I fear I have been much to blame in all this. I never should—

RACH. There, father—let us talk no more tonight. I am weary. Tomorrow, perhaps—

CAPT. Perhaps—

RACH. Good-night. [*Kisses him tenderly*]

CAPT. Good-night. [*Kissing her. She goes to door, turns, looks at him, smiles*]

RACH. Good-night! [*She exits. Captain looks after her, thinks a moment, goes to fireplace, throws pipe into fire, puts hands into breeches pockets.*

Crosses down to R.H. corner, turns and meets Reuben and Roanoke, who have entered from L.H. door. Reuben throws himself on settee; Roanoke crosses and throws himself into upper seat in chimney corner. Reuben and Roanoke very dejected. Music dies away]

CAPT. Been to the city again, eh, Reuben? You quite live there now!

REU. Well, what's the use'n a feller distributin' himself around in pieces. My heart's over there—an' I dunno's I care much what comes o' the rest o' me!

CAPT. Seen Dorothy?

REU. Yesterday. Shouldn't a' come back ef I hadn't.

CAPT. Well?

REU. Well—they'r goin' to send her to England to be eddicated.

CAPT. Sir Frederick has established his claim, then?

REU. Yes. All the papers have arrove from England, an' they've settled that he is her father and entitled to her custody. [*Dorothy's music begins*]

CAPT. Was the mystery of the mother cleared up?

REU. Yes! It appears that Sir Frederick fell in love with her mother who was what they call over there, of low birth, for her purty face. After they was married he was ashamed of her—his family refused to hev anything to do with her—and so he pensioned her off in a leetle seaport town, an' then neglected her. After Dorothy's birth, failin' to get any satisfaction even for her baby, she concluded to leave him and England forever, sellin' what few trinkets she had. She managed to get to America, an' after sufferin' God knows what, died, as we all know. An' now they'r a'goin' to send Dorothy over for some other Lord knows who—to do the same by her! Dorothy says I must be patient an' it'll come out all right in the end. I try to be—an' I hope I shell be, but I tell ye, Captain, it's pretty hard to ring a hog's nose a'thout the hog's a'squalin'!

DOR. [*Putting head in R. door*] Anybody at home? May I come in? [*Enters with a clear ringing laugh*]

ALL. [*Rising*] Dorothy!

DOR. [*Entering like a sunbeam*] Yes, the same old Dorothy. [*She is elegantly attired, wears locket*] In a little handsomer frame, perhaps, but I hope that doesn't alter the picture. They wanted to change my name as well as my dress, but I told them that Dorothy I was and Dorothy I would remain to the end of the chapter! [*They all stand silent*] Why, what's the matter with you all? [*Laughs*] Not afraid I've brought the plague with me, are you? Captain, aren't you glad to see me?

CAPT. Why, Lady Shelton! [*Half jesting*]

DOR. [*Laughing*] Lady Fiddlesticks. Here—[*Shakes hands*] call me Dorothy and say you are glad to see me if you don't want to be cashiered for neglect of duty!

CAPT. [*Laughing and shaking hands*] Dorothy, I *am* glad to see you!

DOR. That is a little more like it! [*He is about to drop her hand*] Here! Here! Here! [*Puts up lips to be kissed. He kisses her. They both laugh*] Now, Roanoke—[*Her manner changing to Roanoke, who has crossed down R.H., offering his hand, which she takes*] What have you to say?

ROAN. Only that the heart of Roanoke is sad, for he knows that another land than that which gave him birth claims the Little Primrose for its own, and that the tall ship will soon spread its white wings to bear her afar over the bosom of the mighty water, where she will be lost to him forever.

DOR. [*Looks at him sadly—tries to speak—she cannot. Her eyes fill with tears. She drops his hand and her head, surreptitiously brushes a tear from her eye, then quickly turns, all smiles, to Reuben. Roanoke goes back to fireplace*] And there's my boy—looking as if he'd lost *every* friend he had in the world! [*Laughs*] Here, Reuben—kiss your mother! [*He does so*] Do you call that a kiss—you naughty boy! There! [*Kissing him*] And there! [*Kissing him*] And there! [*Kissing him—laughs*] Now let me see if your buttons are all right. [*Looks him over*] Yes, for once—I declare—all right! Who will take care of you when I'm gone, I wonder? I'm afraid you'll go buttonless to bed many a night, my poor boy—with no Dorothy to—[*Tries to laugh. Looks up at him, sees a tear on his cheek, takes his face in both her hands, kisses the tear away and nestles to him in the old, old way*] Reuben, don't—don't cry—speak to me! Hold me in your arms as you used to do when I was a little child and there was no *other* father to come between us. Help me to be brave. Reuben, don't you see that I am trying so hard—that I am not happy? That I am only pretending? That my heart is breaking? [*Bursts into tears—gives up entirely and sobs on his breast. Enter Sir Frederick in military cloak. Stops at door*]

SIR F. You forget, child, that you are my daughter!

REU. [*Still holding her*] Forgettin' seems to run into the family, Sir Frederick. You forgot her mother was your wife.

SIR F. [*Wincing*] I committed a grievous sin! I have never ceased to repent it! I shall do my best to repair the wrong I did the mother by justice to the child.

REU. It's a kind o' pity ye can't repair one wrong a'thout doin' another, hain't it? Pity it couldn't a been done years ago, afore the little tender vine had twined itself in an' out around the limbs an' branches of the old oak till they became one. Ye must chop down the oak now to free the vine.

Sir F. [*Abashed*] I shall settle a fine allowance on you. You shall be well paid for all your care and trouble.

Reu. There's some things that can't *be* paid for, an' love's one on 'em.

Sir F. [*Trying to excuse himself*] It is for the girl's good—wealth, station, name—would you deprive her of all these?

Reu. No. You have the right to take her, an' it's for her good that she goes. The last's the argyment that silences me. I hain't a'goin' to stand agin that.

Sir F. 'Tis useless to prolong a scene painful to us all. To me, whose sin has been its cause, more painful than to any here! Captain Winslow—[*Taking his hand*] pardon me. I leave my daughter with you till the morrow, when I will either call or send for her. Duty demands my immediate departure. Good-night.

Capt. Good-night.

Sir F. [*Going, turns, looks sadly at Reuben and Dorothy, says kindly but with much dignity*] Good-night, Mr. Foxglove. [*Exit. The moon has slowly risen by this time. It lights the exterior; the fire, the interior*]

Rach. [*Entering from R.D.*] Father, there is—[*Sees the group. Her eyes catch a glimpse of Dorothy. She springs forward*] Dorothy!

Reu. [*Staying her*] Hush! She's sobbed herself to sleep! Ef you don't mind, I'll set here an' hold her awhile. She's dreamin', mebbe, an'll be glad to find herself in my arms when she wakes. [*Takes her in arms and sits on settee with her head on his breast. Music changes. Enter Dyke Hampton, pale and haggard, his dress awry, hair dishevelled. Has the appearance of a man who has ridden hard and had a terrible struggle with himself. He does not notice Reuben, Roanoke or Dorothy. Rachel looks frightened; Captain surprised. Dyke stops at door as if afraid she would not be there*]

Dyke. [*Speaks hurriedly and with passionate effort to be calm*] Rachel Winslow, I rode from this spot resolved never to see you again. I rode hard. I struggled fearfully with myself. But as I spurred my panting horse into the thickness of the night, I seemed to see you in another's arms. At the sight all the fiends of darkness seized my struggling soul. I struggled longer, in vain. I turned my horse's head and lashed him on. He lies dying at your door. I entered fearful lest I should find my vision true. I cannot—I *will* not, give you up!

Capt. Dyke Hampton, listen to me!

Dyke. Captain Winslow—listen to me! [*Furiously*] She loves this Wynthrop! I know it now, and so do you! [*The Captain is taken aback at this*] Your word is pledged to me. Keep it. Give her to me—or tomorrow sees her homeless and you a beggar! [*As Dyke comes down, Reuben lays Dorothy on *settee—motions to Roanoke, who comes down noiselessly. Reuben commits Dorothy to his care and quietly exits*]

CAPT. [*Almost paralyzed, doubting how to act or what to say*] I—I—

RACH. [*Calmly*] Father, let me speak. [*Crosses to Dyke*] Dyke Hampton, I do love Mr. Wynthrop. You, I never can love! Take me but as I am and I will become your wife.

DYKE. [*Amazed, springs towards her*] Rachel!

CAPT. [*Turning her around*] No! I'll be damned if you do! I am an old man, worn out, it may be, with hard service, but hand in hand we'll go forth into the world. You shall not give your hand to one man while your heart is wedded to another.

DYKE. [*Worked up to a paroxysm of rage and disappointment*] Then go forth to beg—to starve—for, by my soul, you sleep not another night under this roof. I might have guessed as much when that canting, hypocritical scoundrel became your guest! A man of whom no one knows aught—who is, if the truth were known, a fugitive before the law—hiding in the dark, afraid to show his face in the broad light of day!

NED. [*Springing through door*] You lie, you hound—you lie!

RACH. [*Rushing to him*] Ned!

CAPT. and DYKE. [*Astonished*] Ned?

NED. Yes! Ned Farnsworth! [*Dyke staggers back, thunderstruck*] Do you know me now, you craven cur? The boy your coward hand struck to the earth—from whom has sprung the avenging man to pay you back ten-fold the blow you gave, and who will not rest till your foul carcass swings from the gallows tree! Murderer!

ALL. Murderer?

DYKE. [*Livid with rage*] Take care—

NED. Yes, murderer—the murderer of this old man's son!

CAPT. Merciful Heaven, can this be true? [*About to fall. Ned and Rachel run to him*]

NED. Look to your father. [*As Ned turns his back, Dyke quickly draws pistol and fires at Ned. Roanoke, who has been watching him, seizes his arm, the pistol is discharged in the air. Dorothy awakes—is dazed. Reuben enters hastily, carrying gun—speaks in loud whisper. Change music and keep up till end of scene*]

REU. Silence, every one an' ye! Eight hundred British soldiers under Pitcairn are a'marchin' to seize the stores an' ammunition at Concord—see—[*Points. All the characters, who have stopped in exactly the positions they were in when he entered, now crane forward without moving their bodies, to see. The moon is now very bright, and the British soldiers are seen marching silently past window from R. to L. Instant's pause*] The hour for action has come at last. Ned, where's your horse?

NED. Fastened under the shadow of the great oak.

REU. Mount like litenin'! Rouse the Minute Men as you go! We must be there afore 'em.

CAPT. Rachel! My gun! [*She exits—re-enters with gun and powder horn —gives them*]

DYKE. [*Who has been watching his chance, makes rush for the door*] Ah! Rebels! Not yet! Ho! There rebels!

REU. [*Seizes him by the throat*] Silence, or ye'll never speak that word again! [*Thrusts him back*] Roanoke, take charge of that yelpin' wolf! If he moves, strangle him! [*Roanoke stands guard with folded arms*] The Committee of Safety's assembled at the house of Jonas Hundel in West Cambridge. If surprised they're lost. Who will warn them?

DOR. [*Springing down*] I will!

REU. Brave girl! Mount Brown Winnie. [*She starts off R.*] Don't spare the lash! Ride for your life!

DOR. [*As she exits*] I will!

REU. [*Arms aloft*] And now, God of Battles, inspire this, the first blow for *American Independence.* [*All kneel except Roanoke and Dyke. At same moment Ann Campbell appears on stairs with gun*]

PICTURE

Second picture: Dyke and Roanoke in same position—Ann back to audience, guarding door with gun, ready—Rachel kneeling and clinging to her, but on her R.H. Close in with SCENE 2—*"The Stand at Lexington." Lexington Green in 1775. See historical picture. Enter Reuben marching on twenty men in double column, followed by Ned and twenty men in same manner. As they reach positions.*

REU. Halt! [*They do so*]

NED. Halt! [*They do so*]

REU. Ned! Talk to 'em.

NED. [*Stepping to the front*] Comrades! The hireling soldiers of an obstinate and audacious King are at last marching through the peaceful villages of Massachusetts to seize by force of arms, confiscate and destroy, our property, invade and lay waste our homes! Not content with depriving us of every right granted us by charter, with taxing the very air we breathe, with closing our ports, removing our seats of government, quartering his soldiers on our people, he has, in a speech to his corrupt ministers in Parliament, declared us rebels—outlaws—and set a price upon the heads of those who dare to resist his mandates! To us will belong the imperishable, the priceless honor of repelling the first advance of those armed marauders, of striking the first blow for a *Nation's* life!—a blow that will resound from Ocean to Ocean—find a welcoming echo in every true American heart—heal discord—cement our cause—encourage the timid—strengthen the brave—till the nation, rising as one man, will fight while a single arm remains—fight till the glorious cause is won and the last invading soldier has left our shores! Be firm—be true—be brave—and we cannot fail!

REU. Here they come. Steady! Steady! There's a heap on 'em, but don't be skeered! Let them shoot first! Wait for the word—but when you do shoot, shoot to kill! Steady, I say! [*Enter L.1.E. British Grenadiers and Light Infantry, all bayonets fixed. They form L. of stage.* NOTE: *The Americans have all sorts of guns, and not above five with bayonets*]

COL. SMITH. Disperse, ye rebels! Disperse! Throw down your arms and disperse! [*Dead silence*] Fire! [*First platoon fires—retire. Second takes its place. No one falls*] Rebels! My soldiers fired over your heads. The next volley will be at your hearts! Again I say disperse! [*Silence*] Ready! [*His men get ready*] Lay down your arms and disperse! [*No answer*] Fire! [*They do so and several Americans fall, among them Reuben, who at once springs to his feet*]

REU. Fire! [*The Americans fire. Several British fall. The Americans retreat, carrying off their dead*]

COL. SMITH. Load! [*The men, who have discharged their pieces, now load with great precision*] I think that's given the Yankees all they care to have. About! [*They do so*] March! [*They exeunt L.1.E. The church bells now begin to ring an alarm. Men, Women and Boys, in all manner of costume, some just from the plow, a Blacksmith, etc., etc.—some without coats, some without hats. Some have guns. Blacksmith has sledge, Farmer has axe, etc., etc. One Old Man hobbles on, on crutches. An Old Woman gives him a gun and powder horn. He hobbles off R. Boy runs on—gives Man a gun. Wives and Husbands embrace, kiss, etc. Some of the Women go off crying—others cling to their Husbands—others go on to the fight with them—all silent and determined. No confusion. This scene must be dressed, rehearsed and acted from pictures. Enter R.H. Dorothy. She has the appearance of having ridden all night*]

DOR. Men! Men! For the love of God—hasten! There—there—[*To a Woman who has a Baby in her arms and who is clinging about her Husband's neck*] Woman, is this a time to stay your husband? Brave men! Brave men! Quick! Quick! On to Concord! Every arm is needed now! [*To a Boy who rushes past with a gun*] Well done, young hero! Oh, no—King George, you'll never conquer iron hearts like these! [*Distant cannonading*] Hark! Artillery! They are reinforced. Haste, or all is lost! [*Cannonading—booming —bells—fife and drum—distant musketry, etc., etc.*] Quick! To a peerless victory or a glorious death! [*Hurries them all off and exit R.H. See all ready for*]

BATTLE OF CONCORD

[*When in full blast, change to* SCENE 3—*"The Concord Fight." To be rehearsed and arranged from plates and as will prove most acceptable; practicable and effective, and*]

ACT III.

TIME: *June 1775.*

SCENE I: *Mystic River. This scene represents a regular log fort. Supposed to have been built during the French War as a protection against Indian surprises. Large logs well chinked with mud. It is roofed and is set so as to show exterior action on L.H. of stage and is built to burn—fall to pieces and blow up during action of play. Long rifle over chimney place. Reuben discovered in rocking chair, head bandaged. Ann Campbell setting cooking things to rights. Characteristic music at rise.*

ANN. There! I think that'll do agin the Captain and Rachel comes!

REU. Hes the skins arrove?

ANN. Yes. This mornin'. Mr. Farnsworth ses there's commissary stores for a month. He's gone now to fetch the folks. How in the name of Ephriam did you find this 'ere place anyhow?

REU. Didn't find it. It found us. Ned and me's hed to do consid'able skirmishin' o' late an' one night found us in a dense pine wood—it was so dark you could scursely see yer hand afore ye. We darsn't build no fire afear o' Injuns, so we laid down at the foot o' what we supposed was a huge rock to wait for daylight. It rained cats an' dogs in the night. In the mornin' we found that we'd been a'makin' a dam of ourselves to keep the water from runnin' under this 'ere cabin. After cussin' ourselves for a couple o' natural born suckers an' findin' the place was deserted, we took possession on't in the name of the Continental Congress.

ANN. I've heard o' folks that didn't know enough to go in out'n the rain, but I didn't think you was one on 'em.

REU. [*Laughing*] We named it Fort Farnsworth. We've made good use of it since. It's a safe place to hide sich ammunition an' stores as we come across. We've got a bar'l o' gunpowder an' about a ton o' lead under this floor now!

ANN. Mercy on us! Where?

REU. [*Laughing*] I thought you wan't a'feared o' powder?

ANN. No more I hain't, when it comes straight agin me from the inside of a gun! But I don't keer to cook my vittals with it.

REU. There ain't no danger. This 'ere powder's too well brought up not to know when to go off! It can tell a Red Coat or a mean Injun as far as you can smell a skunk! You can't make it kill a Yankee no how!

ANN. I wasn't born in the woods to be skeered by an owl—but I'll whistle Yankee Doodle everytime I sweep this floor—for all that!

REU. [*Slyly*] I wouldn't do that ef I was you—the British whistled that tune marchin' to Concord an' they run so all-fired fast gittin' back that they hadn't breath enough left to whistle fer a dog!

ANN. Concord! Ef I'd only been there to see it! It's jist like showin' a red flag to a mad bull to talk to me about them British! [*Thinks to herself a minute, then suddenly with both hands on hips*] Say, Reuben, I'd like to 'list.

REU. 'List?

ANN. Yes—'list! They've called for men—hain't they?

REU. Thirty thousand's got to be riz' in New England—13,000's Massachusetts' share—I'm one o' *them!*

ANN. An' I'm another!

REU. You! [*Laughs*]

ANN. Yes, me! It won't be the fust time a woman's wore the breeches!

REU. [*Slyly*] Did you ever wear 'em, Mrs. Campbell?

ANN. No! But I kin—an' I hain't the only woman that kin an' will ef her country's to be served by doin' it! Jist let Congress call for women, an' ef I don't raise a rigiment on 'em that'll lick Satan out'n the same number o' Red Coats an' make 'em wear petticoats arterwards, my name hain't Ann Campbell! That's all. [*Dorothy's music*]

REU. [*Smiling*] I'll mention it to Colonel Ward the next time I see him. [*Dorothy heard singing off stage L.*] There's a recruit for yeou! Now I'd like to command a regiment o' them! Handsome as a picter on dress parade an' truer'n steel in action! [*During this Dorothy has sung herself on stage so that she is at the door by the end of Reuben's speech. She carries a pail of water*]

DOR. [*Outside door, laughing*] Pull your chairs away! I'm coming. Quick! [*Puts head in—laughs*] Ah—I caught you! [*Enters with clear ringing laugh. Reuben chuckles. Ann pretends to be angry*] What makes you blush so? [*Laughs*]

ANN. Dorothy Foxglove! D'ye mean to say I'm a'blushin'? Why, I'd think no more a'settin' up clus to Reuben then a hen would a'layin' a egg! [*Dorothy's music ceases*]

REU. What d'ye want to deny it fur? Ye know ye had yer arms around my neck! [*Chuckles*]

ANN. Reuben Foxglove, ef that was the fust lie ye ever told it'd a'choked ye! [*Smiling at the thought of the past*] It's a good long time sense I had my arms around a man's neck, and I dunno's I'll ever git 'em there agin—but if I *do,* they'll *stay* there for the balance o' my nat'ral existence. So put that in yer pipe an' smoke it fur tobaccy! [*Exit a la militaire, R.D.*]

DOR. [*Who has placed the pail on bench and has been listening with a pleased expression—fills a gourd with water and comes to Reuben with a laugh*] Here, take a drink of water to rinse that down with. [*They both laugh*] And how is your poor head today?

REU. On my shoulders, thanks to you, Dorothy! [*Drinks water. Dorothy replaces gourd. Music to bring on Ned, Rachel, Roanoke and the Captain*]

DOR. Nonsense! I only did what any other mother would have done for her sick boy. [*Laughing*] Once you were so helpless, Reuben, you didn't have ambition enough to even lose your buttons. [*Laughs*] And now, sir, I'm going to make you a nice pan of hot biscuit for your supper. [*Going to R.D.*]

NED. [*Off stage L.*] Yes, rather difficult, but all the safer for it!

DOR. [*Stopping*] Hark! Mr. Farnsworth's voice. It's Rachel! [*Runs to L. door and throws it open. Rachel enters. They embrace*] Rachel—dear Rachel! [*They retire up R.H. Dorothy relieves Rachel of things and gives them to Ann, who has come on R. door. Ann takes the things off R. Captain Winslow enters. Reuben rises and shakes him by the hand. Takes Captain's gun and places it against chimney. Roanoke enters and after placing gun against wall U.L. corner, turns to talk to Ann, who has entered and crossed over to table with materials for mixing bread. Ned enters and leans his gun against wall L.H.* NOTE: *All Ann's entrances and exits in this Act must be a la militaire—all her movements and actions the same*]

REU. [*As if continuing conversation with Captain*] Yes, thank'er, Captain, 'bout as good as new, I reckon. [*Cease music*]

NED. There, Captain! And you, Miss Rachel, welcome to Fort Farnsworth. [*To the Captain*] We thought this would be the safest place for you till matters cleared up a bit!

CAPT. [*Bowing his head and then taking a survey of the premises*] Comfortable enough and capable of resisting quite a siege!

Ned. Built during the French War, I should judge, as a protection against Indians. You see, we have the loops and all the requisites—[*Pointing to them*] of a first-class fort. [*Laughing*]

Capt. If these old logs could speak they might tell strange tales of the past. Who knows?

Ned. Reuben, are you able to report for duty?

Reu. Able an' willin', Ned. My ole legs's been idle so long, they're twisted up like a skein o' yarn.

Ned. Then come along! [*Reuben gets up*] There's glorious work afoot. We meet a few friends at the old place. Roanoke, it is important that we are not surprised! You understand?

Roan. The dog is not more faithful—the fox more cunning—the eagle more vigilant! [*Takes up gun*] Fear nothing.

Ned. Ladies, are you afraid to be left alone till evening?

Dor. We are soldiers' daughters, Mr. Farnsworth!

Ann. [*From table*] An' I'm a soldier—don't yeou forgit *that!*

Ned. There is not much danger of our retreat being discovered—still caution is never to be despised. I would advise barring the doors and shutters and not stirring abroad till we return.

Dor. [*Laughing*] Ah, you'll find us safe and sound. Never fear! [*The men all exit L., carrying their guns—Roanoke last. As he gets to the door he casts a long, lingering, hungry look at Dorothy. Their eyes meet. She smiles and inclines her head to him. His face lights up and he exits joyously. Music dies gradually away and changes to distant march, which is kept up now working with scene till Lieutenant Smollet is on stage and scene with Dorothy well begun, when it dies away*] Now, Rachel, you sit there—[*Places her in rocking chair*] and tell me all the news, while I—[*Turns and sees Ann getting dough ready*] Now, Mrs. Campbell, I thought I was to make those biscuits! Here, now—you just give me that apron. [*Takes apron off her*] And if you've anything else to do, go and do it! [*Laughs*]

Ann. Well, as you'rn my superior officer I reckon my duty is to obey. [*Salutes and marches off L. Rachel and Dorothy laugh*]

Rach. Our home has been seized and, at the instigation of Dyke Hampton, an order has been issued for the arrest of my father on a charge of treason. The soldiers are now in search of him. If he should be taken, I tremble for life!

Dor. They'll not find him. Mr. Farnsworth is a match for twenty Hamptons!

Rach. I pray for his safety but a little while longer. Congress has appointed George Washington, Commander-in-Chief of our armies. He is expected in Cambridge within a month to take command. My father, who fought with him under Braddock, will seek a position on his staff.

DOR. And you—[*Rolling dough*]

RACH. I'll remain where Ned thinks safest and best till his duty permits him to call me wife!

DOR. He's handsome, isn't he? I love to look at a handsome man. That's why I'm so fond of looking at Reuben. [*Laughs. Six Soldiers, "British," headed by Smollet march on from L. and range behind house*] Well—if I were a man—Hush!

SMOL. [*Outside*] Halt! Two of you guard the right hand. [*Two do so*] Two the left. [*Two do so*] And two this window. If any person attempts to enter or leave the premises, arrest them. If they resist—fire!

DOR. Lieutenant Smollet! [*Startled*] They've tracked your father. If he sees you, all is lost—in there—and leave me to try and baffle him! [*Rachel exits R. Dorothy sings and busies herself with the biscuits as if nothing had occurred. Smollet puts head in at window*]

SMOL. Beg pardon! I'm in search of—[*She looks up*] Lady Shelton!

DOR. [*As if surprised*] Lieutenant Smollet! [*Laughs*] You are just in time to help me with the biscuits! Come in. [*He does so*] Sit down. [*He does so*] I'm delighted to see you! Excuse my not shaking hands. [*Showing hands—all flour*] Now, make yourself perfectly at home. Well, well, this is a surprise! [*Smollet is a trifle weary*]

SMOL. Lady Shelton!

DOR. Dorothy Foxglove—if you please!

SMOL. Miss Foxglove—[*Bowing*] I cannot say how delighted and pained I am to meet you again—pained because I come on an unpleasant duty. [*Placing hat on bench*]

DOR. Indeed! Does it concern me? [*Working—not looking*]

SMOL. It does! I am ordered to arrest and convey you to your father. [*She stares, but instantly recovers*] Also, to arrest Mr. Foxglove on the charge of abducting one of his Majesty's subjects.

DOR. [*Furtively looking around as if for means of escape—then changing to laughing manner*] But he did not abduct me—I abducted myself!

SMOL. Beg pardon! I have my orders.

DOR. What if I refuse to accompany you?

SMOL. You will compel me to use—[*Very respectfully*] force!

DOR. [*Must show that she is thoroughly frightened and only trying to find a way out of the dilemma*] What? Carry me off? Wouldn't that be romantic! Well, I must get these biscuits ready for supper before I go, at all events!

SMOL. Where is Mr. Foxglove?

DOR. I do not know.

SMOL. On your honor?

DOR. On my honor.

SMOL. [*Bowing*] Are you alone here?

DOR. No. My friend Rachel Winslow and Mrs. Campbell are in that room. [*Points to R. door*]

SMOL. No one else?

DOR. If you doubt me, order your men to search.

SMOL. Miss Foxglove, I will subject you to no indignity I can avoid, believe me! [*Bowing*]

DOR. [*Bowing*] Thank you! [*Aside*] If I could but detain him till the men return!

SMOL. [*Who has been taking a survey of the premises*] I wish this duty had been assigned to another!

DOR. [*Coquettishly*] Do you—really?

SMOL. [*Embarrassed*] Well, that is—I don't exactly—

DOR. Since I must be *carried*—[*Coquettishly*] off by some one, I know of no one I'd prefer to you.

SMOL. [*Amazed*] Thank you!

DOR. [*Who has gotten a pan of biscuits ready*] Please put this on the hearth. [*Giving him pan. He obeys without thinking what he is doing*] Thank you. Do you know you used to say a great many pretty things to me?

SMOL. Did I?

DOR. Did you mean them?

SMOL. Well—I—

DOR. Oh, dear! I forgot to cover the pan. Please put this over those biscuits—[*Giving cloth. He takes it, same manner*]

SMOL. [*Very much in love and showing it*] I was going to say—

DOR. [*Simply*] You once told me you loved me.

SMOL. [*Confirmatively*] I did.

DOR. Here. This is ready. [*Giving him another pan. He takes it as before*] Did you mean it? [*Hands him another cloth*]

SMOL. [*Covering the bread*] From the bottom of my heart!

DOR. [*Finishing work at table—wiping hands clean*] Do you love me still? [*Coming down—Dorothy L.—Smollet R.*]

SMOL. Yes!

DOR. Prove it!

SMOL. How—by getting down on my knees? [*Laughs*] My men! [*Points to window*] Rather an undignified action under the circumstances—don't you think so?

DOR. I'll close the shutter. [*Does so*]

SMOL. Ask something else—I beg!

DOR. [*Getting close to him—finally drawing his arm around her waist and toying with his hand*] Go back to Sir Frederick and say your search was unsuccessful.

SMOL. Miss Foxglove, you were never more charming. It breaks my heart to refuse you—but—

DOR. You *do* refuse?

SMOL. Positively! [*Decidedly*]

DOR. I think I like you better—I certainly respect you more—for it.

SMOL. I'm sure you do.

DOR. Then I presume I must go with you. But I shall need close watching! If I can escape, I will. [*Laughing*]

SMOL. Decidedly! All's fair in love and in war, you know!

DOR. [*Laughing*] Do you remember the day I decorated you with apple parings?

SMOL. I shall never forget it! [*Laughs*]

DOR. [*Coquettishly*] You used to call me your little Captain.

SMOL. And shall be proud to do so still!

DOR. Does it become me? [*Putting on his hat*]

SMOL. Everything becomes you! It is a pleasure even to be the object of your sport! [*Music till picture formed by Ann and Rachel*]

DOR. I wonder if you have forgotten our drill. Let me have your sword. [*He gives it*] Now! Attention! [*He stands in position*] Heads up! [*Coming close to him*] Lieutenant Smollet—[*Laughing*] You are my prisoner! [*He laughs. She at once changes her manner and says in low quick decisive tones*] If you attempt to move but as I dictate, I'll send a bullet through your brain. [*Throwing away sword and quickly snatching pistol from his belt, cocking it and pointing it at his head*]

SMOL. [*Realizing*] My dear Miss Foxglove—

DOR. Attention! [*He does so. She speaks in hurried whisper*] Order your men to stack arms and enter. And remember, the slightest sign and you are a dead man.

SMOL. [*Deeply chagrined—hesitates—then concludes to obey*] Corporal, call in your men! Stack arms and enter. There is a mistake here! [*The two Men on guard L.H. go behind house. All are heard to stack arms. Then they enter, single file—range across back of stage and face audience*]

DOR. Bar the shutter! [*Smollet does so*] Take your place there. [*Places him C., facing audience. He folds his arms. She takes position in front of him, back to audience. Pistol aimed*] And remember, I am a determined and desperate woman! [*To Soldiers who are now on*] Soldiers, as your officer tells you, there *has* been a slight mistake here. He came to take me prisoner. I have turned the tables on him—that's all! [*Soldiers look at each other an instant—then at the Lieutenant—and realizing the situation, start R. and L. as if to recover their guns. At the same instant enter Ann R.D. with soldier's gun and fixed bayonet, and Rachel same way from L. They rush down and form a line in front with Dorothy. Aim at Soldiers. Picture. Cease music*]

ANN. I'm 'listed at last! Three cheers for the first regimint of American women!

DOR. Lieutenant, order your men to remove that trap and go below!

SMOL. [*Without looking*] Corporal! Obey! [*Corporal directs men—they remove trap and go below—the Corporal last. He makes a dart at Ann. She presents the gun*]

ANN. I know a trick worth two of that. Go below! Go below! [*He finally does so*] Now shut up the shop! [*He closes the trap*]

DOR. Lieutenant, give me your word not to attempt to escape or release your men, and you are at liberty!

SMOL. You have it!

DOR. Guard's relieved! [*Rachel puts up gun*] Forgive me, Lieutenant—[*Offering hand cordially*] But all's fair in love and war, you know! [*Music till Reuben and party on*]

SMOL. [*Hesitates—then laughs—takes hand*] You've fairly won, Miss Foxglove, and, upon my word, I'm not half sorry either! [*Dorothy, Rachel and Smollet retire. Ann marches on to trap—goes rapidly through the manual of arms—then marches up to C., puts down gun—marches off R.—returns with guns—places them beside hers, and continues quickly till all the guns on—keep last gun and stand sentry on trap door. This business will be new and very fine if done right. Enter Reuben, Ned, Captain Winslow, Roanoke and two Woodmen—all armed*]

REU. Well, Dorothy, how about them 'ere? [*Sees Lieutenant—aims gun quickly. The others act also, but in different positions*] Ah! A surprise!

DOR. Yes!

REU. Ah! [*Movement*]

DOR. [*Quickly and springing in front of Smollet*] B—but for the Lieutenant, father—not for us!

REU. What in the name of Satan—[*Ned has crossed to Rachel, U.1.R. She is telling him. He laughs*]

DOR. You shall see. Sergeant Campbell!

ANN. Private, if you please! High private's good enough for me!

DOR. Private Campbell—[*Ann presents*] Bring forth the prisoners.

ANN. [*Throwing up trap*] Rats! Come out'n yer holes! [*Soldiers come up. She points. They range down R.*]

DOR. You see, father—Lieutenant Smollet was detailed to take you and me prisoner.

REU. Well! Be we took?

DOR. No! I relieved him of the disagreeable duty!

REU. Wa'al b'gosh! [*The Soldiers look at each other and smile. The Woodmen slap each other on the back and shake hands*] How in natur—

DOR. You shall know all—in good time. [*During this scene Ann has paced up and down in front of Men as sentry*] The question now is the disposal of these men!

REU. Ned! What'll we do with the critters?

ANN. Give 'em to me for target practice!

NED. [*To Lieutenant*] How did you discover our retreat?

SMOL. Mr. Hampton gave the information to Sir Frederick on condition that he would use it to secure Mr. Foxglove and his daughter only. [*Reuben's party all look at each other*]

NED. Captain—[*To Winslow*] there's more in this. What do you advise?

CAPT. Bind them! [*Reuben, Ned, Roanoke and the two Men bind the Soldiers with withes*] Allen, you two take them by the circuitous route to the place from whence we have just come. Use caution. Report at once to Colonel Ward. [*Smollet comes down to him and holds out hands. Captain smiles*] No! No! Lieutenant, you will remain with us and make yourself as comfortable as circumstances will permit!

SMOL. Thank you! [*Bows. Over, joins Ladies*]

CAPT. [*To the Men*] Forward! [*Allen stands at door and points off. The Soldiers exit and off followed by Allen and Herrick as they are going*]

ANN. Let me go with 'em, Captain. They may need another man!

REU. [*Coming down to her*] Say, don't yer forgit this regimint's got to eat! An' you're cook!

ANN. Cook! That settles it! No use'n a feller tryin' to win martial glory here! I see that! [*Puts gun against wall and exits R. door very dejectedly*]

REU. Captain! Ned! There's danger ahead! [*Music till end of act*] Dyke Hampton's tracked us out.

CAPT. Well, what then?

REU. Don't you see? First git rid o' me'n Dorothy—then secure Rachel, murder Ned an' kill you if necessary—or I'm a double-headed Dutchman!

NED. [*With decision*] Reuben is right. We must not remain here! [*It has gradually grown dark outside and in. Ann re-enters as if to set table*]

ROAN. [*Who has been listening*] Silence. Stir not till Roanoke returns.

[*All stand in exactly the positions they were in, as if straining to catch the slightest sound. Roanoke exits noiselessly, but swiftly. Listens with ear to ground and suddenly but silently darts into the woods and disappears. He is gone about ten seconds when he as silently and swiftly re-enters—bounds into the cabin and bars the door. Reuben quickly bars the other*] The White Panther and his Renegades!

REU. Dyke an' his Injuns—by thunder!

NED. Quick, let us escape before we are surrounded!

ROAN. And fall into the ambush of the cunning Panther! Hark! [*Indian heads are now seen darting from all parts of the scene. They are hideously painted*]

REU. Ned! [*Aside to him, but so as to impress the audience*] How's the tide?

NED. [*Same manner*] Full.

REU. Then we're in for it. There'll be fightin' enough now, I reckon! [*At the word fighting, Ann, who has been listening, springs and gets her gun*] How many ar'em, Roanoke?

ROAN. The Renegade is a coward! He will not attack an equal foe. The ear of Roanoke deceives him not. He outnumbers us ten fold!

REU. Let's draw the Panther's claws a bit!

ALL. How?

REU. I'll show ye an' all Indian fighter's trick! [*Takes off coat—stuffs blanket in it to make dummy—breaks broom handles for arms. All in cabin busy themselves in this so as not to notice action outside of cabin. Reuben gets long poker from chimney place. During this enter cautiously from behind house Dyke and Morton Handy, a renegade white man in Indian dress. It is quite dark now*]

DYKE. You got the barrel of rum I sent?

HANDY. Yes, or I wouldn't 'a been here.

DYKE. The soldiers have doubtless gone with Foxglove and his daughter. That leaves but the Captain, the old woman Campbell, the girl and—[*Between his teeth as if he could not bring himself to speak the word*] her lover. Batter down the door. Fire upon the men. Do as you will the women. But the girl—harm not a hair of her head. Place her alive—alive, within my arms —[*Passionately*] and then ask of me what you will!

HANDY. Trust me! I'll do my best!

DYKE. Good! Remember—Rachel alive to me! [*They retire*]

REU. [*All being ready*] Here, Dorothy. You work this Fandango—go—Rachel, you open the shutters. Boys, yer muzzles to your loops and wait for the word! Now!

SMOL. Mr. Foxglove, I am an Englishman and your prisoner. But I am also a soldier. Will you permit me to assist in protecting these ladies? [*Spoken quietly and with dignity*]

REU. Lieutenant, you're—a—man! Give him a gun!

SMOL. I have one, thank you. [*Quietly, as if it were an every day occurrence. Dorothy looks gratitude. Smollet knows it, but seems not to*]

REU. Silence all! Ready! [*Rachel opens half the shutter. Dorothy works dummy out of window. At same instant a volley from all sides followed by the Indians who rush out to scalp body*] Fire! [*Ann, Captain, Reuben, Ned, Roanoke, fire. Three Indians on L. fall dead. The others disappear. Dorothy hastily withdraws dummy. Rachel blockades window*] Well done, my beauties! Load quick, lads! Dorothy, tend to Trusty while I reconnoiter. That kinder staggered 'em, I reckon! [*They all load. Dorothy loads Reuben's rifle. Ann and Smollet take Soldiers' guns. Reuben at loop*] They're goin' to batter down the door. All on this side! [*Men do so and get ready*] Study-y- [*Twelve Indians appear bearing large pine trunk as a ram—it is very heavy. Two others creep around from behind house placing brush, etc. When the ram is near enough, the men swing it backwards and forwards several times to give it an impetus*] Fire! [*Six Indians fall. The balance drop the ram and disappear. Four are killed of the six who fall, the other two regain their feet and stagger off badly wounded*] Good boys—load! Here, Dorothy—[*Gives her gun. Places eye to loop*] Give me a gun! Quick! [*She gives him Soldier's gun. At that instant an Indian darts out from L. with pine knot lighted. Reuben fires. The Indian falls*] Another gun! Quick! [*Before they can get it to him, another Indian rushes on, snatches torch from dead one and fires the house. A tremendous yell and the Indians swarm around the fire*] They have fired the fort! We're lost! [*All stand aghast*]

SMOL. Throw open the doors—[*Very coolly*] and let us fight our way through them!

CAPT. That were certain death to us—and to these poor *girls* a fate *more* terrible!

REU. [*In hoarse whisper*] There's one chance for us—an' but one! Ned! Quick! [*Ned disappears down trap. All seem to exclaim "Thank God"*] There's an underground passage that fills an' empties with the tide! If the tide's out—we're safe. If not—[*Ned appears*] How is it, Ned?

NED. On the turn! There's a chance! [*All faces light up*]

REU. Quick, then! [*Ladies are passed down first. Captain, Roanoke, Smollet and Ned follow. Reuben keeps guard till the last. As he is going*] If that fails—the gunpowder! [*Descends and closes trap. Meantime the Indians have gathered around the house with guns ready to shoot when the people shall be forced to appear. The house falls in with a crash. The Indians fire a volley and yell. Dyke Hampton and Handy appear. Picture*]

DYKE. Damnation! They have escaped! [*Terrific explosion. The scene is blown to pieces and amid the din, smoke and yells, and groans of the dying and wounded Indians, the Curtain descends*]

ACT IV.

TIME: *June 1775.*

SCENE 1: *On Mystic River. Picturesque landscape at daybreak. Distant hilly country very fair and beautiful on R. Water of creek supposed to flow in from river—sort of cove L. The sun rises during action of scene and must be very fine or not done at all. Two boats moored on beach. Camp fire and kettle R.1.E. at which are seated Reuben and Ned. They are in tatters. Reuben no coat or hat. Ned part of coat and hat. The idea to be conveyed is that the explosion had almost stripped them. Ann Campbell with man's coat and hat on, gun between knees, asleep against large rock R.C. Dorothy and Rachel asleep on blanket spread on stage L.C. Rachel covered with an old skin—wolf; Dorothy, by what is left of Smollet's coat. Smollet in shirt sleeves, shirt torn, no hat, hair and beard awry—one boot, this very much the worse for wear, is seated L., tying up other foot in colored silk handkerchief. Roanoke on ground C. Allen with Reuben. Allen no coat or hat. Ann has them. Captain asleep L.1.E. Music at rise. Dies out as scene well open.*

REU. [*As if continuing conversation*] Wa'al, ye see the dumed thing went off sooner'n I kalkelated!

NED. Why didn't you tell us you were going to fire the powder?

REU. There wa'ant no time to talk. Allus stretch yer legs accordin' to the length o' yer coverlet. Dyke wanted a bonefire 'n I thought I'd give him one. I laid the train from my powder horn as I went along an' soon's I see the Captain 'n Roanoke 'n the wimmen in the boat I let'r rip!

NED. You took a desperate chance, Reuben!

REU. Got to when the odd's agin ye. Ye can't ketch no trout a'thout wettin' yer feet. I wa'ant a goin' to hev them cut-throats foller us if I could help it!

SMOL. They will never again follow anyone in the world.

REU. There's no danger o' our meetin' 'em in the next. I giv 'em a ticket clean through to the other side, I reckon. Come—[*Rising*] all rise. Let's see how breakfast's progressin', Lieutenant. After breakfast you are at liberty to depart. Tom Allen'll show ye the nearest way to your command.

To-night yer men'll be sent to join ye. An' if ever ye get into trouble an' we kin help ye out, call on us an' ye'll find us there. [*Offers hand*]

SMOL. Thank ye, Mr. Foxglove. [*Taking hand*] I shall regret to leave you all, however.

ANN. [*Asleep*] That's it! Giv it to 'em! Second section—forward!

REU. [*Smiling*] The Brigadier's at it agin! [*All listen*]

ANN. Ready! Present!

REU. [*In her ear*] Fire!

ANN. [*Jumping up and pointing gun first at one and then the other*] Come on, durn ye! I ken lick a regimint on ye! [*All laugh. She realizes the situation. Joins in laughter*] What'n thunder'd ye want to wake a feller up for? I'd a captured the hull British army'n another minit!

REU. We kind o' hed pity on 'em, ye see! [*Reuben, Ned, Roanoke and Allen, carrying their guns with them, start off L.1.E.*] Come along, boys. [*Exeunt*]

ANN. [*To Smollet*] Where be they a-goin'?

SMOL. To look after breakfast.

ANN. Oh! I was afeared they was a skirmish afoot an' they wanted to leave me behind! I'll be glad when we git inter the reglar army. I'm sick a'cookin'! [*Going off carrying gun. Looking back and talking to Smollet, stumbles across the Captain*] Mercy on us! [*Sees who it is*] Beg pardon, Captain! [*Exit L.1.E.*]

CAPT. Don't mention it. [*Gets up quite stiffly. Stretches and yawns*] Hello, Smollet, that you?

SMOL. Minus a boot and other articles!

CAPT. [*Seeing girls asleep*] Girls not up yet, eh?

SMOL. Heard them snoring as I passed their room just now.

DOR. [*From the blanket*] *Never* snored in my life! [*Sits up laughing*]

SMOL. Beg pardon. Meant figuratively, of course! [*Laughs*]

DOR. Rachel—let's get up!

SMOL. [*Naïvely*] Shall I retire?

DOR. If you're sleepy.

SMOL. I mean—to permit you ladies to rise.

DOR. [*Laughing*] We can rise without your permission. Here, give me your hand! [*He does so. She jumps up*]

SMOL. Shall I assist you, Miss Winslow?

RACH. No—thank you. [*Jumps up laughing. Sees Captain. Goes to him*] Good-morning, father.

CAPT. Good-morning, my daughter.

DOR. Excuse me. Good-morning, Captain.

CAPT. Good-morning, Dorothy, child. [*Rachel and Captain L. Dorothy at blanket. Smollet R. of her. Rachel and Captain talk together and finally saunter off L.1.E.*]

DOR. Lieutenant, come and help me make this bed!

SMOL. With pleasure. [*They fold up blankets*]

DOR. Allow me. [*Offers to help him on with his coat*] That's the first red coat I ever wore.

SMOL. Did you find it comfortable?

DOR. Extremely so!

SMOL. Continue to wear it.

DOR. [*Archly*] The colors might run.

SMOL. Warranted fast.

DOR. [*Archly*] *How* fast?

SMOL. [*Same way*] *Stead*-fast! [*Turning and offering his arm*]

DOR. [*Singing and putting the coat on him*]

Steadfast and true
I'll prove to you
If you'll follow me, over the sea! [*Laughs*]

SMOL. I return to my regiment today.

DOR. Do you? [*Half seriously*]

SMOL. [*Sadly*] Yes. What shall I say to Sir Frederick?

DOR. [*Archly*] Tell the truth! [*He looks at her. Their eyes meet. Both laugh*]

SMOL. I mean—concerning you!

DOR. [*Laughing*] Say that I am all right!

SMOL. You are relinquishing a grand position.

DOR. I am retaining my liberty—and the wealth of honest hearts that love me!

SMOL. Your title is—

DOR. One of which I am very proud—an American Girl! [*Smiling and bowing*]

SMOL. [*Resignedly and offering hand*] Perhaps we may meet again.

DOR. I hope so. [*Seriously*] Believe me! [*Takes his hand*]

SMOL. We're friends. [*Smiling*]

DOR. [*Looking him fairly in the face, as if to undeceive him as to any hope beyond*] Yes—friends. True, honest friends! [*They look at each other a moment, then drop hands*]

SMOL. [*Quickly*] I wish I could find my other boot. [*Limps. Enter from L.1.E. Reuben*]

REU. Now then, Lieutenant. Hello! Dorothy, up and dressed!

DOR. Not much dressing to do, father. [*Looks at him comically*] Whatever will you do now, child! You've no buttons to lose!

REU. Borry some o' the Brigadier's! Come along to breakfast. Lieutenant, escort her to the dinin' hall. [*Exit Reuben, L.1E. Music very lively till Smollet and Dorothy off, then change to bring Dyke and Handy on and off, then change to bring Roanoke on. Keep up through his scene and change again and keep up till end of Act*]

SMOL. [*Limps over to her—places hand on heart, bows very low and offers arm. She accepts with great ceremony. He limps off, steps on pebble, business and exit. Music changes. Enter Dyke Hampton, Morton Handy and Two Indians from U.E.L. Dyke is bruised and wounded almost beyond recognition. They have no guns*]

DYKE. You must be mistaken.

HANDY. No! How did ye say he came here? [*Laughs outside L. by Reuben and Party. Not too loud*]

DYKE. With a band of Mohawks. About ten years ago. When they left he went with them, but one day suddenly returned. He seemed fascinated with the place, as a strange dog will sometimes be—disappearing one day—returning the next. They all took kindly to him, and so he's lived among them ever since.

HANDY. Then, I'm not mistaken. I've not seen him for eighteen years, but I'll swear to his face.

DYKE. So—you lied to me!

REU. [*Outside*] Three cheers for the Brigadier! [*All laugh*]

HANDY. [*Avoiding the question*] I told you I'd put him out o'way, and I believed I'd done it. I give him to a Mohawk chief who for a portion of the money you give me promised I'd never hear of him agin—but it's him. The fates seem agin ye, Dyke! Best give this thing up.

DYKE. Never!

SMOL. [*Outside*] No! No! No!

DOR. [*Outside*] Yes! Yes! Yes! [*All laugh*]

HANDY. It's cost a good many lives already.

DYKE. What's a few Indians? I live and while I live I'll not give her up. I love her. [*Handy laughs*] Yes, love her. And I hate that man. I'll kill him and have her, if all Hell stood between us! Once in my possession I'm her Master! [*Dorothy sings a line and ends with a merry laugh. Handy's eyes light up with passion*]

HANDY. Dyke! I've got a cage that'd just fit that singin' bird. I want her!

DYKE. [*Appalled*] That's dangerous. She's an English Colonel's daughter.

DOR. [*Outside*] No! I'm not!

HANDY. [*Lecherously*] I must have her! [*They look at each other*]

DYKE. Take her. Now to our places. This time we'll *not* fail! [*Exeunt from whence they came, Dyke last. Music changes. Enter Roanoke, gloomy and despondent. Seats himself on rock R.C.*]

SMOL. [*Outside*] What I mean to say is—

DOR. [*Outside. Laughing*] You've said quite enough! I'll not hear another word. [*Runs on laughing*] I'll—[*Sees Roanoke. Runs to him*] Why, Roanoke—are you ill?

ROAN. No. Roanoke is not ill. He is sad. [*She coils herself down at his feet and leaning on his knees, looks up into his face*] Very sad! He must say farewell.

DOR. [*Alarmed*] And why?

ROAN. The English officer loves the Primrose.

DOR. [*Looking at him half laughing, half frightened, trying to draw away*] Why, Roanoke, you're jealous!

ROAN. [*Seizing her fiercely and restraining her*] As the Tiger of his mate! Roanoke loves—but his skin is dark! His race wild, untutored, savage! His birth unknown. His very tribe a question!

DOR. But safe and gentle of nature—strong of arm and brave of heart. He is a Man! All are not such who wear a fairer skin.

ROAN. The English officer is brave.

DOR. As a lion!

ROAN. And noble!

DOR. As a Prince!

ROAN. Does the Primrose love him?

DOR. I—[*Casting down eyes*] I—you—

ROAN. Does the Primrose love him? [*Fiercely*]

DOR. You frighten me! [*Springs up. Gets away from him*]

ROAN. [*Going up stage to R.*] Forgive. Roanoke will not harm. He will wander away into the depths of the silent forest from whence he never should have emerged. He will seek the tribe from which he never should have strayed—and never shall the shadow of his life fall athwart the sunlight of your path again.

DOR. [*Going to him and almost unconsciously drawing him back to his seat and resuming her position*] All sunshine and no shadow would wither and kill the sturdiest flower. How then could the fragile Primrose hope to survive its fierce rays?

ROAN. Other forms will shelter, other arms protect, other eyes bedew it!

DOR. Roanoke will not leave us—[*He looks at her*]

ROAN. He must!

DOR. His country?

ROAN. He has no country.

DOR. His friends?

ROAN. He has no friends.

DOR. [*Half laughing—half crying*] What! No Reuben, who has loved him as a son?

ROAN. [*Impatiently rising as if not to acknowledge it*] No!

DOR. For—[*With wild cry*] my sake—[*Frightened the moment she has spoken. Change music*]

ROAN. [*Catches her in his arms like a whirlwind. She tries to resist. All useless*] You love Roanoke—[*At that instant enter Herrick U.E.R. Carries gun. Speaks like lightning as he enters. Distant cannonading which continues all through scene*]

HER. Reuben! Farnsworth! Quick! Quick! [*All enter from L.1.E.*] Prescott and Putnam are fortified on Bunker's Hill and Howe with all his force is marching to dislodge them! [*Ann rushes off L.1.E.*]

REU. Dorothy, a kiss—[*She rushes to him, is clasped a second in his arms. Captain and Ned have kissed Rachel*] Come, Ned! [*Going R.U.E.*] Concord and Bunker's Hill!—

NED. [*Following*] Will leave a record to the world! [*Exeunt Captain and Herrick, follow quickly*]

ROAN. [*Quick as lightning to Dorothy*] Roanoke protects you!

DOR. Protect our country first. If you live, return to me. [*Roanoke stares—bethinks him of his gun. Starts L.1.E. to get it. Meets Ann, who has rushed on with hat, coat and gun. Seizes her gun—quick struggle. He throws her off. She almost falls as he exits R.U.E. with gun. Distant rumbling of cannon all the time. The scene must be played with lightning's rapidity. Rachel and Dorothy have gone up R. to look after men*]

ANN. Well, durn your copper colored carcass! [*Enter at same time Dyke, Handy and Two Indians—no guns. Dyke has large knife in belt. Dyke seizes Rachel from behind and pinions her in his arms. Handy seizes Dorothy same way. An Indian seizes Ann same way and bears her to left corner. Other Indian strikes Smollet on head with tomahawk and fells him, then rushes to assist Indian with Ann. As he nears her she kicks him in the stomach. He turns a complete somersault—recovers quickly. Women scream*]

DOR. Help! Father! Roanoke!

RACH. Help! Help!

DOR. Roanoke!

ROAN. Here. [*Bounds on like a panther. Snaps gun at Handy. It misses fire. Throws away gun and springs for Handy's throat. Handy lets go*

Dorothy. Indian drops Ann and seizes Dorothy. Handy and Roanoke meet C. A terrific struggle for the supremacy—a la Lorna Doone. During it Smollet recovers and is seen to steal off. Handy has Roanoke by the throat and is strangling him]

DOR. Roanoke! [*Seeing him nearly overpowered*] I love you! [*At the sound of her voice Roanoke gathers superhuman strength and is in the act of overpowering Handy, whom he now has by the throat, when Rachel, scarce knowing what she does, breaks from Dyke, seizes knife from his belt, rushes down to stab Handy. He adroitly turns Roanoke so that she stabs him. With a cry he relinquishes his hold on Handy and falls. Dorothy breaks from Indian, runs to Roanoke and takes his head on breast, passionately kissing and calling on him to speak. Rachel stands transfixed with horror*]

HANDY. [*Quickly recovering himself*] Rachel Winslow! You have killed your brother. [*Rachel shrieks, stands like one mad, then faints. Indian catches her*]

DYKE. [*Springing down, catches Handy by the throat, as if to choke the words back*] You lie! You lie!

PICTURE AND CURTAIN

[*Change music to Yankee Doodle. Boom the cannon. Discharge musketry, etc., etc., and ring up when all is ready on*]

SECOND PICTURE

YANKEE DOODLE

[*See Plate. When all ready they march to R. Change music and change to*]

THIRD PICTURE

BATTLE OF BUNKER'S HILL

[*See Plate. Part action, part tableau. Reuben, Ned, Captain on promenade. All the cannons, guns and drums and*]

RING ACT DROPS

ACT V.

TIME: *1776.*

SCENE: *Dorchester Heights. Same scene as Act I—except to have house further off stage to give more room for tableau at end. Discovered: Captain Winslow smoking and seated on rustic seat L. Rachel in low rocker sewing. Music at rise.*

CAPT. Yes—my dear daughter—this is indeed a glorious day for us and for our cause. The British at last compelled to evacuate our city and leave our people once more to the enjoyment of life, liberty and happiness!

RACH. And you, dear father, restored to the wealth of which you had been so willfully deprived—blest by the discovery of a son, long mourned as dead—

CAPT. Possessing the love of a daughter whose courage and devotion have never faltered! It needs but the success of my country's arms to make a peaceful ending to an eventful, active life!

RACH. You have positively reconsidered your determination of entering the Army?

CAPT. Yes. I am old—and a cripple. You will be alone. I don't know how a piece of an old soldier like myself can better serve his country than by protecting one of her fairest and bravest daughters!

RACH. Oh, father!

CAPT. No word from Ned yet, eh?

RACH. No, father. He said he would not return till he brought undoubted proofs of dear Harry's identity—and Hampton's villainy.

CAPT. Oh! I've no doubt of Roanoke's identity at all. There was always a something that seemed to draw me towards him! Handy's story—the scar over the right eye caused by the fall he received when a baby—the unmistakable likeness to his dead mother—are all proofs positive that he is my son. Still, I presume that for the Law's sake, it is right to establish the fact beyond question.

RACH. What a strange fatality was that—that impelled me to rush to his aid—and so nearly made me the instrument of his death! [*Peculiar strain for Roanoke's entrance—kept up till his exit*]

CAPT. Fatality, indeed! 'Twas that blow—struck as he believed fatally—that caused Handy to cry out in his savage joy, "You have killed your brother!"

RACH. The Hand of Heaven, father! Let us acknowledge its wisdom and power. [*Enter U.E.L. Roanoke in full Continental uniform—"Private"—followed by Reuben dressed as Continental Sergeant*]

REU. Well, Captain—here we be! How d'ye think the boy looks in his regimintals?

CAPT. Look! [*Enthusiastically*] Like the hero he is sure to prove himself—like the soldier it gladdens the old man's eyes to look upon! God bless you, my boy! [*Embraces Roanoke, crosses to Reuben wiping eyes*] God bless you, my boy!

RACH. [*Embracing Roanoke*] My dear—dear *brother!*

ROAN. Sister! Father! [*Taking hand of each. Then looking up reverently*] *Mother!* Strange—sweet words to the Indian's tongue! Had Roanoke known them sooner—he might perhaps have prized them more! But now there is another and a dearer—*Wife*—the great spirit has no gift to equal that!

REU. Look here—if Dorothy loves you—

ROAN. Roanoke knows she loves him! [*Crosses to Reuben*]

REU. Then, all's I got to say is—it'll be purty durned hard work to keep ye apart. She's little, but by Mighty—she's slicker'n a fox. I allus found out —that ef she would—she would—an' ef she wouldn't all Natin couldn't make her!

ROAN. Her father—

REU. See here—don't yeou go to stealin' a feller's privileges! I'm her father a good deal more'n he is!

ROAN. Keeps her prisoner!

REU. There ain't no more prisoners in Boston—that is evacuation day— an' ef she don't give 'em a slip I miss my guess!

CAPT. Come, my son. Calm yourself. All will yet be well! Come into the house.

ROAN. Roanoke cannot dwell within walls like a caged animal! He must be free to come and go at will! He will wander toward the great city. He may meet her. Should he do so and they deny her to him—let them beware the Indian's fury! [*Strides out majestically, raising himself to his full height, 1.E.R.*]

RACH. [*Clinging to the Captain*] How fierce he looked, father! He terrifies me. Can this be my brother? [*Music dies out gradually*]

CAPT. I almost doubt—myself—I never saw him so before. Perhaps his wound—[*Offers arm to Rachel*]

REU. That's it—his wound—not the one Rachel give him though. Dorothy's wounded him her—[*Points to heart*] an' he's cut deep too—he is!

CAPT. I fear he will never learn—never be able to accustom himself to our ways. [*Going L.2.E. with Rachel*]

REU. Give him a chance—ye can't expect to make a white man out'n an Injun in a day! Time'll fetch him around all right.

CAPT. I hope so!

REU. I know so! I know Injuns—I do! [*Captain and Rachel exit. Ann enters from house. Stops on steps at seeing Reuben and holds up both hands in delight*]

ANN. Well, Reuben Foxglove! An'—*in*—yer *new rig-i-mintles,* as I'm a sinner! [*Comes down*] Turn around an' lets hev a look at ye. [*Turns him around*] Well, ef you hain't stunnin'! I'd give the hull balance o' my life to wear that suit jist five minutes by the watch!

REU. [*Slyly*] Come into the Dairy 'n I let ye try 'em on!

ANN. [*Paying no attention to that*] Them's the kind o' clothes for a feller to fight in! No petticoats a'flappin' round a man's legs to trip him up! *So—that's* the new uniform, eh? [*Her eyes fairly dancing with admiration*]

REU. Yes! We've took the swaddlin' clothes off'n the child Independence and dressed him in Continentals—no more creepin' for him. He's got to walk alone now! An' afore King George knows it he'll walk clean through the British Armies—ownin' *and controlin'* every foot of this—*the Land that give him birth!*

ANN. Ef a feller wa'ant a woman what fun he could hev'n them clothes!

REU. Ye got a leetle the wust b' the last skirmish didn't ye, Brigadier?

ANN. 'Twa'ant no fair fight—no how!

REU. What was it the Injun said to ye?

ANN. Wanted me to go to his wigwam an' be his squaw!

REU. Did ye go?

ANN. I hain't yit! I'm a'waitin' till he comes round agin!

REU. An' so Lieutenant Smollet got ye all out'n the scrape—eh?

ANN. Yes—he managed to crawl off unobserved—an' jest as Hampton thought he had us all in a hornet's nest—he surrounded us with a party of his own soldiers an' took us all prisoners!

REU. All on ye?

ANN. All but Dyke! He jumped into the river'n by swimmin' under water escaped. Smullet marched us all afore Sir Frederick who give orders to have Roanoke's wounds seen to—an' all on us released except Dorothy. The Injuns an' Handy he turned over to a guard! I tell ye, Reuben, that Smullet's a good 'un! If ever I do go to a wigwam to be a squaw, it'll be with a man like Smullet! [*Dorothy's music*]

REU. Say, Brigadier! I've been a'thinkin'—that ef you'n me—that is, ef we was to form ourselves into a platoon—[*She looks at him in perfect amazement*] ef we was to—[*Tittering laugh heard from bushes R.*]

ANN. [*Hearing it*] What's that?

REU. Woodchuck, I reckon. Here, take my arm ef ye're skeered! [*She does so*] I was a'thinkin'—[*Laugh heard again*]

ANN. [*Stopping*] Reuben, that wa'ant no woodchuck!

REU. 'Twas a squirrel a'chatterin', then—[*Listens*] I was a'thinkin'—[*Laugh heard again*]

ANN. There it is agin! [*In loud whisper*] Reuben Foxglove, there's somebody a' listenin' to ye!

REU. [*In loud whisper*] There hain't!

ANN. [*Same manner*] There is too! I'm so shamed—I'm blushin' all up an' down my back. Hark! [*Music swells*]

DOR. [*Unable longer to restrain—bursts into a loud peal of laughter and appears from behind shrubbery, followed by Smollet. Ann gathers her clothes up around her and makes a comic exit. Reuben stands shame-faced. Dorothy rushes to him and clasps him around the neck and kisses him. Smollet enjoys the scene*] Oh! You dear darling old dad—and so you've been and gone and done it! How delightful! Would you believe it, Lieutenant—that boy—that child—actually in love and never let his mother know a word about it! [*Laughs*] But I'll pay you up for it, sir! [*Shaking finger at him*] But I'll *take you away* from her. [*Laughs*] She shan't have you—there! She's a designing minx—that's what she is! She has taken advantage of my absence to lead you away! I always told you to beware of the female sex! Here—hold up your head—[*Laughs*] Now, tell me the truth. What was she saying to you? [*Music dies away*]

REU. She wanted me to go to her wigwam an' be her squaw! [*Dorothy and Smollet laugh*] Dorothy—don't say anything about it, will ye? [*She laughs*] Ye needn't laugh. You know how it is yerself!

DOR. Well, I shan't. [*Patting his cheeks*] It shall fall in love if it wants to —and its mother won't plague it—a dear—darling—old popsey-wopsey! [*Laughs*]

REU. [*Looking kind of sheepish*] It was kind o' mean to sneak in on a feller. [*Laughs*] Lieutenant, I thought you—

SMOL. Don't blame me, Mr. Foxglove. I only obeyed orders!

DOR. [*Turning Reuben around*] Let us look at you! What a lot of buttons! What fun you will have losing them! [*Seriously and nestling up to him*] You won't let anyone but Dorothy sew them on, will you father?

REU. My darling—there's nothin' on this earth'll ever take your place in old Reuben's heart—be sure o' that. [*Lifting her face between his hands and kissing it*]

DOR. [*Nestling*] I like that! [*Then quickly changing*] Where's Rachel? I'm dying to see her. Lieutenant, please find her for me.

SMOL. Certainly. [*Crosses to house and exits. Roanoke's music*]

DOR. Father—[*Smiling and hesitating*] I want to tell you something. [*Clasps her hands and hesitates*] It's a great secret—but, oh, such a sweet—happy secret! I'm—[*Roanoke enters R.2.E.*]

ROAN. Primrose!

DOR. [*With a scream of joy rushes to his arms*] Roanoke!

REU. [*Smiles to himself*] Ya-a-s—a great secret! [*Exits into house*]

ROAN. Roanoke feared he had lost his sweet Primrose forever—

DOR. She told him she would come. Did he doubt her?

ROAN. He doubted those who took her from him—but he holds her in his arms once more. [*Fiercely*] They shall never tear her from them again. [*Music dies out*]

DOR. Tut! Tut! Tut! You must not look so fierce—[*Laughs*] Remember you are not an Indian any more—and your name is not Roanoke—it is Harry! [*Laughs*]

ROAN. [*With disgust*] Laugh! The name of a baby! Roanoke is a mighty name.

DOR. [*Repeating as if to taste the words*] Roanoke is a mighty name. [*Half to herself*] I love it. Let me look at you. How handsome you do look in your fine uniform—and yet I do not know but that you were grander in your old savage dress!

ROAN. [*Starting to go*] Roanoke will put it on again!

DOR. No! No! No! [*Laughs*]

ROAN. Roanoke, too, loves it best. It was for her he put on this. [*Dorothy's music*]

DOR. And for her must he wear it to the end! It is this uniform—covering hearts like his—brave, honest hearts—that is destined to give the world its mightiest Nation. Bring—[*Laying hand on coat. Then sadly*] or send this back to me—stained—worn—bloody—if need be—and I will worship it and you—my Indian—soldier—hero—husband in life or death!

ROAN. Roanoke hears! [*Proudly*] His heart beats! His veins swell! His breath comes thick and fast! He pants to show the Primrose what brave deeds he'll dare for her sake!

DOR. And now Harry—[*Laughs. He gives her a look. She corrects*] Roanoke—sit down. [*Seats him on old plow—comes around and seats herself between his knees. Throws head back and arms around his neck*] I am going to introduce you to a person you have hitherto ignored but whose close acquaintance and friendship it will be very necessary for you to court in the future—I am going to—[*Laughs*] introduce you to the first pronoun—I—[*He looks as if he could not comprehend*]—say—I—love—you!

ROAN. The Primrose loves Roanoke!

DOR. No! No! No! [*Laughs*] You—love—me!

ROAN. Roanoke loves the Primrose!

DOR. [*Laughs*] How stupid! Here! Repeat—just what I say. Understand? [*He tries to comprehend*] Say—I understand!

ROAN. [*Face lighting up*] I understand! [*Pleased*]

DOR. That's right. [*Delighted*] Now say after me—I—

ROAN. I—[*Pleased with himself*]

DOR. Love—

ROAN. Love—

DOR. You—

ROAN. You—

DOR. Capital! And I will—

ROAN. Capital! And I will—

DOR. [*Laughs and continues*] Obey you in all things!

ROAN. Obey you in all things!

DOR. Good!

ROAN. Good!

DOR. Hush! [*Puts hand over his mouth*] Now listen and do not speak. [*Changes her whole manner*] My father will be here today.

ROAN. [*Fiercely—jumping up as if comprehending the meaning of the visit*] No! No! He shall not—

DOR. [*Soothing him*] Hush! [*Smiling in his face*] You promised to obey. [*Changes manner again*] He is my father—and during these past few months that I have lived with him, he has been so kind—so good—so gentle—he suffers so terribly for the wrong he did my mother—he loves me so dearly and he is so sad and lonely—that I have grown to pity—to love him.

ROAN. I understand! [*He must change here to broken-hearted submission, all his Indian fire gone*]

DOR. And so—at last I have come to think—that perhaps it is my duty not to leave him to himself. That my mother would be happier in Heaven, were I to help him atone for his sin. That she would look down and even smile—to see us together—father and daughter!

ROAN. [*As before*] I understand.

DOR. We are all called upon at some time to make sacrifices in this world —and I believe we are purer—nobler—holier—for having made them bravely—heroically!

ROAN. I understand. [*As before*] Your father will take you from me.

DOR. If it is his will that I accompany him—

ROAN. You will obey? [*Same tone*]

DOR. He is my father!

ROAN. You will obey? [*Same tone*]

DOR. [*Slowly and sadly—but firmly*] I—will—obey.

ROAN. [*Looks at her a moment—then raises his hands to heaven—and in a sudden heart-broken burst—cries—*] My God! My God! My God! [*Bursts into tears and his head falls on his breast*]

DOR. [*Awe stricken, almost afraid to break in on his grief*] Roanoke!

ROAN. [*Without looking up*] Roanoke no more! [*Hoarse whisper*] That name is lost to him forever!

DOR. [*Winding arm around him*] Roanoke!

ROAN. [*Without looking*] Silence—pity—silence!

DOR. Are you then the only sufferer—have I no heart to surge, to break, to part? Do I not love you? And must I not give you up? [*Bursts into tears on his breast. He takes her in his arms*]

ROAN. Does your father know you love me?

DOR. He does!

ROAN. I understand. The Indian's love would stain.

DOR. Not Indian—you are—

ROAN. Indian by nature if not by birth. He would wed you to one of his own proud people!

DOR. [*With decision*] That—shall he *never* do!

ROAN. [*Quickly, taking both her hands, holding her at arm's length, looking steadily into her eyes*] Promise that!

DOR. [*Firmly*] I swear it!

ROAN. Let me then seek him. I'll not rave. [*Fiercely*] I'll not kill him. I'll beseech—[*Soft*] I'll plead—I'll fall upon my knees and implore him not to part us!

DOR. And if he will not listen?

ROAN. I, too, will obey!

DOR. My brave—lionhearted Roanoke! [*He gazes into her face a moment, then pulls her to his breast and gives her a long passionate kiss. Music changes to lively air. At the same moment enter Smollet from house. She hears his step and turns all smiles*] Lieutenant, I was just telling Roanoke how cleverly you succeeded in bringing me before my father after all! Ha! Ha! Ha! [*Laughs heartily*]

SMOL. [*Laughs*] Ah, it was quite an accident. Hampton really had more to do with bringing it about than I after all. I was going to remark that I've searched the whole house and the only female I could find was Mrs. Campbell and she seemed endeavoring to escape to the roof by way of the kitchen chimney! [*Laughs heartily in which Dorothy joins. Music swells. Enter R.1E. Sir Frederick, Rachel and Captain L.3.E. Dorothy runs to Sir Frederick. Roanoke retires R. Captain comes C. meeting Sir Frederick. Dorothy after embracing Sir Frederick goes to Rachel. They kiss, etc. Smollet salutes, as Sir Frederick enters and, after they take positions, Sir Frederick eyes Roanoke sternly. Roanoke endeavors to read his fate in Sir Frederick's face and fails*]

CAPT. Sir Frederick welcome once more. Allow me to present my long lost son! [*Roanoke advances and bows respectfully; Sir Frederick with much ceremony and dignity. Dorothy watches eagerly and is telling Rachel*]

SIR F. [*To both*] I congratulate you both. [*Then to the Captain—Roanoke turns away disappointed*] My regiment will be the last to leave the city. I obtained through the kind courtesy of your commanding general—permission to pay my respects to you before departing. [*Music changes*]

NED. [*Outside R.2.E.*] No violence, boys! Bring him before the Captain—that's all! [*Enter Ned as Continental Captain—followed by Two Continental Soldiers forcing on Dyke who has on a British soldier's coat and belt, etc.*] Captain, here's a gentleman to see you! [*Ned has bundle of papers*]

CAPT. Dyke Hampton! Look at me! [*Dyke does not*] Ah! You dare not! Your cowardice does you credit. You *should* be ashamed to look upon the man you have so deeply wronged! [*To Ned*] Where did you find him?

NED. We were searching his house and unearthed him trying to burn these papers. He had traded coats with a soldier and was endeavoring to escape that way. But my men were too quick for him. Here are the complete proofs of his villainy—your brother's will—the identity of your son—in the dying confession of the savage to whom he was sold—and the statement of his father acknowledging the misappropriation of your property during your absence! [*Gives papers*]

CAPT. [*To Dyke*] What have you to say? [*Looking over papers*]

DYKE. Only this—I love your daughter. To force her to my arms I did it all. No punishment you can inflict will equal the torture of losing her. Do with me as you will. I'll speak no more.

NED. What shall be done with him, Captain?

CAPT. [*To Sir Frederick*] He wears your uniform, Sir Frederick.

SIR F. [*Shaking his head with contempt*] No! We hold no league with cut-throats and murderers!

NED. I have it—Allen—[*To one of the men*] strip that coat off his back. Give him the blue and buff. If he attempts to shirk the slightest duty belonging to it, shoot him on the spot! [*Music changes. They take Dyke off. Ned goes to Rachel and Dorothy. Sir Frederick and Captain retire. Reuben and Ann enter from L.2.E. not noticing balance of characters*]

REU. What I was a'goin' to say—when we was interrupted that time was —[*She looks stolidly into his face*] that is I've been a'thinkin' that is—now that—[*Desperately*] Say, what's the use a'lyin' when the truth ken be proved agin ye. Ann Campbell I'm—say, be ye ever troubled with cold feet? [*She remains immovable. He puts his arms around her waist and kisses her on cheek. She turns and falls on his breast. Business of Reuben. Drum corps heard in distance. Sees party. Tries to rouse her. She is immovable*] Say—Ann—[*Then to party apologizing, not realizing what he says*] Ann's busted her gallusses an' I'm a'fixin' 'em for her—[*To her*] Say, Ann—they're all a'lookin' at ye!

ANN. [*Recovering, half fainting—half crying*] Let 'em look! I don't care a continental cuss! It's been many a year since I've hed my arms around a man's neck—an' now I hain't a'goin' to let nothin' choke me off! Reuben, I'm yourn, an' I'll stick to ye like death to a nigger an' don't ye *forgit* that! [*Reuben and Ann retire to Dorothy as Sir Frederick speaks. Dorothy's music*]

SIR F. [*To the Captain speaking with severity*] I am determined and it shall not be otherwise. [*Gently*] Dorothy, my child, come here. [*She comes tremblingly. Rachel and Ned to L.U.E. To Roanoke—sternly*] Approach, sir! [*Roanoke does so*] Captain Winslow, I am called to battle for my King and country. To your care I commit my child. Should I fall, here—[*Giving paper*] is that will secure her my name and fortune. [*To Roanoke*] You, sir, love my daughter. Go forth. Fight as bravely in your cause—as be sure I shall in mine. She will watch and pray for your return. Dorothy—[*Taking her to his breast*] be happy! I give you *freely*—give you to the man you love! [*Kisses her, passes her to Roanoke, then looks up and says as if to himself*] Am I forgiven?

DOR. [*After embracing Roanoke, returns weeping for joy, to hide herself on her father's breast*] Oh, father! For now you are indeed my father! [*Half laughing—half crying*] Roanoke—why don't you say something? [*Goes up to Reuben. He takes her in his arms—kisses her*]

ROAN. [*Who has been spellbound*] Roanoke has no words! His voice is in his heart. The silent water is ever the deepest. So be his love and gratitude. Let his eyes speak. Awed by the sublimity of the gift, let him stand dumb in the majestic presence of the giver. [*Dorothy brings Reuben down. Roanoke retires. She has Reuben's left hand—takes Sir Frederick's right. They look at each other a moment. She looks into the faces of both. They look at her, then at each other. They smile. She joins, then kisses both their hands, laughs through her tears and runs up to Roanoke. They go to and receive the congratulations of the rest of the party*]

SIR F. Mr. Foxglove—what shall I—what can I say to such a man as you have proved yourself to be! Take this. [*Offers pocketbook. Reuben shakes head*] Not as a reward—but as a token of my sincere and honest love—[*Reuben still hesitates*] for my daughter!

REU. Sir Frederick, I know ye mean well—but what's the use'n lyin'—when the truth ken be proved agin ye. I love that child. Ef it hain't askin' too much, I'd like to hear ye say *our daughter!*

SIR F. [*Extending both hands. They look steadily into each other's eyes—both affected*] For our daughter's sake!

REU. [*Shaking him heartily by the hand—wiping eyes*] Then, I'll take it. [*Takes pocketbook*] It'll help Ann an' me set up shop! [*They go up arm in arm and join party*] Say, Captain, you ken pay Ann's wages to me hereafter! [*Dorothy and Smollet come down*]

SMOL. I certainly congratulate you, Miss—Miss—[*Smilingly*] What shall I say, Foxglove or Shelton?

DOR. [*Laughing and pointing to Sir Frederick and Reuben who are still arm in arm*] Both! See! [*They both laugh*]

SMOL. Well, really you have the most extraordinary family complications! When I first met you you were the mother of one father and now you are the daughter of two! [*Both laugh*]

DOR. Lieutenant—I am indebted to you for many acts of kindness. How shall I thank you for them?

SMOL. [*Lightly, but with a strata of deep feeling underneath*] Pshaw! I've done nothing any other fellow wouldn't have had himself cashiered for the privilege of doing! The society of a charming lady—[*Bows. She smiles*] is not so often thrown in the way of a poor devil of a soldier that he can afford not to be civil! True—I did at one time hope that you—[*She looks at him appealingly*] Well—no matter. [*Seriously*] I've passed the happiest hours of my life in your company. If I, in return, have afforded you any amusement—

DOR. [*Supplicatingly and smiling*] Pleasure—let us call it pleasure, Lieutenant!

SMOL. [*Looking at her curiously*] Pleasure! Why, I'm content—and if circumstances will only permit—I will dance as merrily at your wedding as if it were my own. [*Bows very ceremoniously. She curtseys very low. Bugle calls "Five" heard in distance*]

SIR F. Hark! That bugle warns me to depart. Farewell! [*Takes Dorothy in his arms, kisses her fervently*]

DOR. [*Clinging to him*] Father! [*Calmly*] Is it right that you go—*now?* Right that you should sever every earthly tie—[*With a desperate effort brings herself to say*] Right that you [*Looking at Roanoke and Reuben, then back to him*] should fight against him [*To Reuben*]—against the husband of your child?

SIR F. Hush! A soldier has no choice. Love is strong, but honor and duty are impregnable. I go. But if I live I will return to pass my days among you—and ask no sweeter resting spot than in a land hallowed by a mother's sufferings—blessed by a daughter's love. [*Drums have constantly increased, are now quite loud. Calcium lights on. All the characters retire L.H. Enter L.U.*

E. Drum Corps playing. They march off R.1.E. Then a company of soldiers with their officers. They march off R.1.E. Cannons boom. Bells ring. Second Company. Same. Drum Corps. Third Company. Yankee Doodle. All the ladies, handsomely dressed, strewing flowers. General Washington on horseback—accompanied by his Generals all made up in character and on horseback. More soldiers. The stage is completely filled. Characters shout. Ladies wave their handkerchiefs. Soldiers all shout. Washington lifts hat. Grand Tableau and]

END OF PLAY

[DRIFTING APART

in its first version, known as]

MARY

THE FISHERMEN'S CHILD

CAST OF CHARACTERS

[*First performance on any stage, The People's Theatre, New York, May 7, 1888*]

Character	Actor
JACK HEPBURNE, *skipper o' the "Dolphin"—rough but honest, with a "failin'"*	JAMES A. HERNE
PERCY SEWARD, *son of a rich mother whom he loves; a good fellow but a trifle sentimental*	H. M. PITT
SILAS CUMMINGS, *"Dep'ty Sheriff, Farmacuterist and Clarinettist"*	C. W. BUTLER
HARRY MERTON, *of Percy's set*	
ALECK SAUNDERS } *two of Mary's fathers*	PHINEAS LEACH
JOSH WHILBECK }	ROBERT ALEXANDER
MARY MILLER, *belongs to the village, the fishermen's child*	KATHARINE C. HERNE
MARGARET HEPBURNE, *Jack's mother*	MRS. CHARLES RAE
MRS. SEWARD, *Percy's mother*	HENRIETTA BERT
HESTER BARTON, *stage struck, wants patronage and endorsement*	VIC REYNOLDS
MISS STANLEY } *of Percy's set*	MAUDE JEFFRIES
MISS FAIRCHILD }	ADELAIDE NELSON
MISS EASTERBROOK }	LUCILLE PEARSON
LITTLE MARGARET, *Mary's child*	LITTLE DOT WINTERS

FISHERMEN, VILLAGE GIRLS, LADIES, GENTLEMEN, ETC., ETC.

TIME: PRESENT DAY.

ACT I. NEAR GLOUCESTER, MASS.

ACT II. JACK'S CABIN, GLOUCESTER.

ACT III. HOME OF PERCY SEWARD, BOSTON.

ACT IV. ATTIC IN TENEMENT HOUSE, NORTH END, BOSTON.

ACT V. JACK'S CABIN AS BEFORE.

ACT I.

SCENE 1: *Near Gloucester, Mass. Fishing village on beach. Wharves, shipping warehouses, etc. on R. Gloucester in distance on R.*

TIME: *August, present day. Sea with fishing fleet at anchor in distance supposed to have arrived before the calm fell. The horizon that hazy gray that betokens extreme heat; heat lightning at intervals. Sea is dead calm. The set is a fisherman's hut R., a little better than its fellows; it is built of the hull of a vessel, has a low porch and step; overhung vines; bench beneath window. On L. old wreck to work and work lights behind. A piece or two of wreckage on shore; bead cloth down.*

Thunder; lightning; clouds and rain all to work during act. Wind and sea to move schooner, three master, to work on, go about, tack, drop anchor. Men to go aloft, furl and take in sail. Boat with men to leave schooner. Row towards shore. Sun shines brightly at rise.

MUSIC.

Aleck and Josh discovered removing bars, etc., from dory, which is beached C.R.; they are rough fishermen about 50, with weather-beaten faces and brown hands. Aleck smokes clay pipe. There is a laugh outside R. by Mary and Hester; they run on, arms about each other's waist. They are followed by Percy Seward, a tall, handsome young man about twenty-three, dressed in elegant yachting costume. Hester leaves Mary, goes to Aleck and Josh, slaps them familiarly on the back; they turn and greet her smilingly, she is a rollicking good-natured girl, dressed plainly but picturesquely and coquettishly. She and the men converse in dumb show; the men point off to the fleet; look at the sea, sky, etc.; she sits on the edge of dory, and swings her heels, Nick sits on hunkers, Josh stands leaning on oar; Nick is spinning a yarn to Hester, Josh listening. They enjoy the scene without interfering with that of Percy and Mary.

PERCY. Really, Miss Mary, I think it quite unreasonable, to say the least, to laugh at my protestations of lo—

MARY. [*Laughing and holding up her finger*] Ah! Ah!

PERCY. Respect, I'm sure I see nothing in my infatuation to laugh at. I do lo—[*She looks at him, he checks himself*]—*admire* you, and why not? Everyone here loves you.

MARY. [*Seriously*] And that is the very reason *you* should not. I am an orphan—poor—ignorant—

PERCY. [*Interrupting*] No! Not ignorant.

MARY. Well, unlearned, except for such learning as one gets from these rough, honest people, among whom it has been my fortune to be born. You say you are rich—I have been taught that the rich are proud—are you proud?

PERCY. Yes—in the just pride that always accompanies wealth when tempered with refinement and good breeding—there are different kinds of pride.

MARY. Well, I too am proud! You say you have a dear mother—who loves you and whom you love. [*Taking his hand*] I honor you for that—I can only love the *memory* of mine—her I have never known—neither father nor mother; my father they say was lost at sea. The shock killed my mother—and I was launched—as I may say tempest tossed, upon the sea of life—an orphan. The fisher folks cared for me, first one and then the other—I was known as "the fishermen's child"; at the age of three years Mrs. Hepburne took me as her own. I have lived here [*Points to cabin*] with her and [*Blushes*] Jack ever since.

PERCY. Yes, I have heard that story and will confess that it was that that first awakened a feeling of lo—[*She looks at him*] I see nothing in it to prevent your listening to me.

MARY. Everything—the fact of my being what I am and your being what [*Hesitates*] you say you are—prevents—say that you are honest and would make me your wife, which—[*Hesitates*]

PERCY. You have no right to doubt.

MARY. [*Avoiding that*] Would it not break the heart of that mother you love—to see you married to the "fishermen's child"—would she be willing to receive me as a daughter?

PERCY. Well—[*Hesitates*] she might not at first—but eventually her love for me—

MARY. There—you see that with all your learning I am wiser than you, in that wisdom born of instinct, and which none possess to such a degree as the child of nature—granting even that your mother—how I love that name! with that holy mother love—before which all other love palls as the dew melts before the sun's hot rays, should cast aside all pride of birth, all thought of station and for her *"boy's"* sake clasp me to her breast in loving welcome—how would it be with you after the first flush of fancied bliss had passed? Would you not tire of your fisher bride—would you not shame to present her to your fashionable friends—blush at her awkward ways and country manners—would you not soon learn to draw comparisons between her and the proud and cultured ladies of your class?

PERCY. No! Never—I swe—

MARY. Hush! Yes—In spite of yourself would come the doubt as to the wisdom of your choice—you would learn to ponder on what *might* have been —the caresses you once so eagerly sought would gradually grow irksome—following this would come coldness—neglect—and finally abandonment—for you perhaps remorse—for me the blankness of despair. Ah! No, best leave the daisy of the field in the field, where the hand of God hath sown it! Transplant it to the hothouse—it will wither—fade, fall and die.

PERCY. You have painted a gloomy picture.

MARY. Let us say a true one. There, let us be friends, you know but little of me—*I* nothing of you save that you have flattered me with your attentions —that you are a gentleman I feel—and as such there is my hand—go back to your city friends, choose from among them one more worthy to share your life than I—and you will one day thank me for having saved you from a step you would have regretted to your dying day. [*Hangs her head silently, brushes away a tear, looks up smilingly, laughs*] Besides, do you not know I am not free, that I am already promised to another?

PERCY. Yes—to Jack Hepburne. Mary—may I call you so?

MARY. Yes, my name is Mary.

PERCY. Is he worthy of *you*—you have drawn a picture of your fancied life with me—have you ever drawn one of your life with him?

MARY. Yes—to live always here, among the rough, kind hearts that have known me from birth—to be the staff of his aged mother's declining years and perhaps to close her gentle eyes in sleep at last—to be a fisherman's wife, true and loyal, to make his home bright and happy with my smiles and cheer him with my love—to bid him godspeed on his departure and welcome home on his return. Perhaps one day to place within his arms a fragile image of himself, to kneel with him and thank the giver of all good for the boon of his bestowal—the greatest in his gifts, the blessing of motherhood.

PERCY. But do you not fear that he—

MARY. May *one* day not return—[*Sadly*] Yes—I have thought of that, not with fear, however, for we fisher folks are not much given to fear—but with a sort of dread—but we are a pious people here—the fisherman's life is a hazardous one at best, and we are taught that "He that giveth also taketh away," and to say "Thy will be done." There are worse things than death in this world.

PERCY. I do not mean sea faring dangers, I mean, pardon me—his love for—

MARY. What he calls a social glass?

PERCY. Yes, I have seen—

MARY. So have I. All our people here drink more or less, they seem to inherit it from their cradles. It is as natural for a fisherman to drink as it is for the fish they risk their lives to catch—

PERCY. Have you then no fears that this pernicious habit may grow upon him and one day wreck his life and yours—yes—even that of the unborn babe of which you just now spoke?

MARY. Hush—please—don't, please don't. I dare not look so far as that. Jack is young, and thoughtless, he is rough, but he is honest as he is rough, he loves me [*Hastily*] that I know, and he has promised me that on the day I become his wife—he will give up drink forever. I believe him, I trust him. I must do so, for do I not love him? But, [*Drying her eyes*] there, there, here I stand chatting with you while his vessel lies in the offing waiting only for the breeze to freshen to bring her safely to anchor, and *him* to his mother's arms. I must in and help prepare his welcome, so good-bye for the present. [*Gives her hand*] Forget all that has passed between us, and please do not refer to it again. Believe me you will find *your life* elsewhere.

PERCY. Mary. [*Seriously, respectfully, and with deep feeling*] I can never forget, I accept the sacred title of friend. Let me think of you in my own odd way, I believe I'm better for having known you, and I hope—[*Corrects himself*] I know Jack will be, *must* be nobler for becoming your husband. And now let me exact one promise, and that is, should the day ever come—which God forbid—that you need a friend, you will seek, as you will surely find, that friend, in Percy Seward.

MARY. [*Deeply affected*] I promise. [*He raises her hand respectfully to his lips; she blushes, bows her head and exits into cottage; he raises his hat; as she is off, he turns away with a sigh*]

PERCY. Heigho! Percy, old fellow, you had best order the *Sybil* to weigh anchor and resume her cruise. I'm afraid this is a bad case. You've met pretty girls before and got away scot free, but I'm afraid the fisher girl has unwittingly meshed you in her net. By George! what a brainy creature she is, and what wisdom for one who knows nothing of this bright, beautiful world, save what is found here in this fishiest of fishing villages. She is a gem, and only needs proper setting to be of great price. After all she may be right. You might tire of her; in trying to polish the diamond we might destroy its lustre. She is happy here, she loves this Jack, and I daresay he loves her in his rough way. Far be it from you, Percy Seward, to cast one shadow across her path. No! No! You are her *friend,* let that content you, and the province of a friend is to stand by when danger threatens, and that you'll do Percy, for you're a pretty good sort of a fellow, although a bit sentimental. [*During this speech Nick and Josh have finished their story and gone off R.U.E. At "shadow across her path" Hester has gone with them as far as the entrance, then returning comes R. of Percy who has crossed L. in meditation; she gets in front of him, stoops, looks up into his face*]

HES. A penny for your thoughts!

PERCY. [*Laughs*] I don't know that they are worth a penny.

HES. Not worth a penny! Of who ever could you be thinking then?

PERCY. [*Laughingly*] Of a very idle, purposeless sort of gentlemanly vagabond—myself.

HES. Oh, Mr. Seward! You're in love, hain't you—ha! Ha! Ha!

PERCY. A natural consequence—with a rich-only-to-please himself in the world young fellow, on the one side, and the sweetest, prettiest girl in the world on the other side.

HES. [*With a low courtesy*] Oh! Mist-e-r-Seward—

PERCY. [*Alarmed*] Good gracious, Miss Barton, I didn't mean you.

HES. Why, you said a rich young fellow on one side and the sweetest, prettiest girl in the world on the other, didn't ye?

PERCY. Yes—I confess I—

HES. Well! Hain't you on the one side and hain't I on tother?

PERCY. Yes—there's no denying that—but—I—I—

HES. There, there—don't stammer, it always puts me in a perspiration to hear anyone stammer—ha! ha! ha! I forgive ye—it's only another image *scattered*.

PERCY. [*Correcting her*] Idol shattered!

HES. Eh?

PERCY. Idol shattered!

HES. Oh! Yes—Idol shattered. I knew it was some kind of a image—I only heard it once—it was in the theater up at the Town Hall, Lampey's Unequalled Dramatic Alliance from the Boston Museum, every member a star, in a carefully selected repature.

PERCY. Repertoire!

HES. I guess so. Six days only, three grand performances daily, mornings at ten, afternoons at two, evenings at eight, admission ten cents, a few very choice seats reserved at five cents extra, change of bill at each performance—special provisions for families from the country desiring to eat lunch in the theater—

PERCY. Why! Of course, they could not eat lunch without provisions—see?

HES. [*Looks at him*] Don't interrupt me—lemonade, popcorn, candies and peanuts, served by gentlemanly attendants—no whistling, stamping or catcalls allowed—did you ever see Lampey's Constellation?

PERCY. Never heard of it before.

HES. Why, you live in Boston, don't ye?

PERCY. Yes—born there.

HES. And—ye—*never—heard*—of—*Lampey's*—Constellation?

PERCY. *Never!*

HES. Don't ye ever go to the Museum?

PERCY. Oh yes! Frequently.

HES. Well—They're from the Museum.

PERCY. I dare say—a very long way from it. [*Laughs*]

HES. You needn't laugh. Lampey's great. I've seen all the constellations that come here—I've seen *Peck's Bad Boy, Uncle Tom, Ten Nights in a Barroom, Alvin Joslyn* and all of them and I like Lampey's in "Alonzo the Brave" better than any of them—but then mebbe you see more actin' in Boston then we do down here.

PERCY. Very likely.

HES. I wish I was an actor. I wish some rich man would fall in love with me and put me on the stage. [*Looks at him archly, laughs*] Lampey says I only needs patronage—what's that?

PERCY. Why, when some person high in position, such as the Governor or President in this country, or the Prince of Wales in England, endorses you and introduces you into his set.

HES. Is the Prince of Wales coming to Gloucester?

PERCY. Not that I've heard.

HES. Because he might endorse *me*—Lampey says the more patronage, good clothes and less talent you have nowadays, the better you'll draw. Si! he won't hear of my going on the stage.

PERCY. Si?

HES. Yes, Si Cummins keeps the drugstore up on the corner yonder, haven't you seen his sign? Silas Cummins, Depity Sherff and Farmacuterist, Manifacter'r, Cummins' Bloodroot, Anti-appetite pills, Cummins' Corn Salve, Cummins' Liver Expander, e-t-c., e-t-c., e-t-c.

PERCY. Oh! Yes, I've met the gentleman.

HES. Well, him and me's engaged, but he's got no soul for high art. Lampey says he's of the world, worldly, but he plays the clarinet beautiful and he could lead the band waggin splendid—who leads the band waggin of the Boston Museum?

PERCY. I don't know. [*Laughingly*] I don't think they have one.

HES. No band waggin! Why how on earth do they let 'em know there's goin' to be a show. [*Silas heard off R. playing clarinet: "The Girl I Left*

Behind Me." Hester hears him, with delight, claps her hands] There's Si! Ain't he splendid!

PERCY. Magnificent! [*Silas plays away quite absorbed, gets down between them, finally sees them, blows a terrific blast in Percy's ear, Percy gives a start, claps his hand to his ears*] Mercy on us!

HES. [*Without moving, smiles complacently*] Oh! Couldn't he lead a band waggin though?

SI. I beg pardon Mr. Seward, jest practisin'.

PERCY. Yes, so I perceive—don't mention it, I beg.

SI. Didn't startle you, did it?

PERCY. Oh! No! Not at all.

SI. [*Patronizingly*] But pshaw! I suppose you've heard musicianers afore?

PERCY. Well, yes, some few.

SI. Ever heer Baily Cross?

PERCY. Never.

SI. He was a powerful musicianer, I've seen him play the trombone and Macbeth the same night. He's dead!

PERCY. [*Aside*] He ought to be. [*Aloud*] Is he?

SI. Yes—Trombone busted in the last act an' blowed the top of his head off. Somebody loaded it while he was on the stage "a ministerin' to a mind deseased."

PERCY. Rather sad!

SI. Yes—it ended the piece! Musicianers are scurcer now. [*Plays*]

PERCY. I wonder, Mr. Cummings.

SI. Cummi*ns*.

PERCY. Isn't there a final *G* to you name?

SI. Not as I've heerd on—say, Hester, is there a final *G* to Cummins?

HES. [*Who has been sitting on bench R.*] Yes! G.R.

SI. Oh, yes, *Gr.* that means gunior—see, my father was old Si Cummins, and of course I'm Si Cummins Gr.

PERCY. Yes, I see. Well, I wonder you don't go to the city. Such talent is wasted here, that is to a certain extent.

SI. Well, I've hed a good many offers, but I'm kind o' tied here. [*Plays*] Think I'd kinder astonish 'em up there—don't you?

PERCY. Oh, I've no doubt of it at all.

SI. [*Playing*] The've hed nothing like me up there.

PERCY. Not just exactly like you—you would be a novelty.

SI. Well, you might speak to 'em when you get hum—I might be indooced, jest for a short while, though I couldn't stop long.

PERCY. No—I think a short engagement *would* be best!

HES. [*Who has been acting to herself now crosses to Percy in an abstracted manner*] "Two souls with but a single thought, two hearts that beat as one." [*Throws herself on Percy's breast, Percy folds her in his arms and kisses her. Silas turns her quickly around to L.*]

SI. Say look a here, ef you've got any more soul than you want you jest give it to me. [*Percy laughs*]

HES. [*Pouting*] Oh Silas, you're jealous.

SI. No, I hain't jealous.

HES. It was only a bit of stage business that I was practising anyhow.

SI. Well, you just practise it on me, I can stand it.

NICK. [*Outside R.*] There she comes mates, see her creepin' on over to the westward. [*Enter Nick, Josh, fisherman and female villagers. Nick has ship's glass, all group in semicircle on R. of stage*]

- - - - -	Josh		Silas
- - - - -	*	Nick	*
- - -	Hester	*	Percy
	*		*

[*Breeze is now seen to freshen and move the sea, gradually growing stronger. Enter from cottage Mrs. Hepburne and Mary. Mary leads Mrs. Hepburne to seat on bench and stands beside her*]

MARY. There mother, sit there, his first thought is sure to be of you, and I wish your face to be the first to greet his eyes.

MARG. Heaven bless you, my child!

NICK. [*As breeze freshens*] There she comes, isn't that a glorious sight! What can cheer the heart of the homeward bound sailor like the breeze that bears him to the mother he honors . . . [*Looks at Margaret*] and the girl he loves [*Looks at Mary, who smiles and bows, glass to eye*] Ha-ah—see—up go the sails, how gloriously they fill, now she weighs, see her stretch her arms like a huge giant after his sleep, she yawns, she struggles, she trembles like a schoolgirl over her first loveletter, now she starts. [*The stage has been all excitement during this—people peering over each other to catch a glimpse, Silas running from one spot to another, and getting ready to shout at every exclamation of Nick's; Mary's face radiant; Hester stands on tiptoe, two of the men make a chair of their hands, seat her in it and raise her up—it doesn't suit —she beckons Silas to come and stoop down—he does so, the men take her hands, she jumps on Silas' back, the men holding her hands, and settles herself to comfortably enjoy the scene*] She's off, here she comes. [*Schooner now works on from L., tacks, goes about, lowers sail, drops anchor*] Huzza! [*All shout. Men on schooner man yards; lower boat. Five men get into boat and row away, finally disappearing behind wreck. All shout and wave hats. Hes-*

ter jumps up shouting, Silas falls, she jumps to stage, all laugh] And now, Hester, clear your pipes for a song of welcome to Jack Hepburne, the best skipper and truest mate that ever trod a deck.

HES. [*Sailor fashion*] Aye! Aye! My hearties, and clear your pipes for the chorus. [*Song and Chorus: as it ends glee is taken up off L., very distant. All listen; it comes nearer and nearer, the sound of oars is heard and the scene is worked up, till at end of glee, the boat touches beach, and Jack jumps ashore. Men in boat cast painter ashore, men ashore grasp it and make it fast to toggle, four men follow Jack. Girls and men all crowd around and grasp hands. Girls kiss their sweethearts. Jack goes directly to his mother, kneels, embraces her*]

JACK. Mother! [*Rises*] Mary! [*Clasps her to his heart and gives her a long passionate kiss. Note: Jack must be tall and manly, handsome, about thirty, reddish brown hair and eyes, must be picturesquely dressed in half sailor, half fishing garb, clothes must be clean and fit him perfectly, supposed to be his holiday suit. He sees Percy, who has crossed down L.*]

Sea

- - - - -
- - - - - Group
- - - - ,
- - - Mary, Jack
Margaret * * Hester
* Percy *
R. Footlights L.

JACK. Hello, a stranger! [*Mary is about to speak. Percy checks her*]

PERCY. Permit me to introduce myself—Percy Seward, of Boston, on a yachting cruise. I dropped anchor in your charming bay, and drifted ashore some weeks since. I have been fortunate enough to make the acquaintance of Miss Miller and your mother as well as these other good people.

SI. Hester, we're the good people. [*Hester nods*]

PERCY. And have found them so entertaining that to tell the truth I have no desire to continue my cruise further. My yacht—

SI. I allus thought that was *yatch*.

PERCY. The *Sybil* lies yonder and is at the service of yourself and friends during my stay.

JACK. [*Offering hand*] Glad to see you, Mr. Seward, and thank ye kindly for your invitation, but after a fellow has had months of the geniwine article he don't hanker much arter playin' sailor. No offense and thank ye all the same. [*Percy goes up, sees Silas and Hester, crosses to them*] Hello Si! [*Shakes hands*] and Hester! [*Kisses her*] Gone play actin' yet?

HES. No, Jack, I'm waiting to be endorsed.

JACK. [*Crosses C.*] Well, mother, and you Mary, you'll be glad to hear that we've had a glorious trip, the finest of weather, the biggest catch of the year, and better than all, to learn that I'm to go no more to sea.

MARY. [*Springing to him*] Oh! Jack!

MARG. [*Tries to rise, cannot*] My boy! My boy! [*Jack goes hastily to her, assists her and holds her in his arms. Mary leans on his shoulder*]

JACK. True mother, my father lost his life in the service of Hemingway & Son—I have labored faithfully for them since I have been able to tell a mackerel from a cod, and for all this I've been given charge of the warehouses here, and there's $300 to be placed in the village bank for me the day that I'm married, and here's the letter that tells the good news. [*Shows letter to Margaret and Mary, they eagerly look over it*]

HES. [*To Silas*] Why ain't you given in charge of something?

SI. I have been, ain't I Depity Sherff of this deestrict? [*During this clouds have gradually darkened the horizon although the sun shines brightly on the stage. Horizon quite dark*]

JACK. So now, Mary, my darling, here in the presence of these, my honest shipmates, whose dangers on the sea I shall no longer share I ask you to name the day that I may call you wife, and—

SI. Collar the $300, don't forget that Jack. [*Omnes laugh*]

MARY. Jack, you have always had my heart, there's my hand. [*Gives it*] Let the day be when you will.

JACK. [*Snatching her to his heart and kissing her. Silas does same to Hester. All the men upstage do same to their sweethearts*] No time like the present —let it be now, send for the parson, [*Boy runs off R.*] run for the fiddler—

HES. No! No! Here's the clarinette. [*Points to Silas*]

JACK. We'll have such a jollification as never was. [*All shout*] Oh, mother, [*Goes to her, kisses her*] Mary, my own, my wife. [*Goes to embrace her. The horizon has become black by this. At the word "wife" a terrific flash of lightning and a crash of thunder. At its sound all the characters who had their hats in hand in act of shouting, pause. Picture of alarm and fear; Margaret springs up in alarm, Mary shrieks and hides her head on Jack's breast; Jack looks alarmed but defiant. Hester alone faces the sea and looks boldly at the storm. Silas hides himself behind her*]

MARY. Oh, Jack, if that should be an evil omen!

JACK. Nonsense. [*Half superstitious himself*] It's but a summer storm, and see how brightly the sun shines on us—what matter the storm, it cannot harm the sea—look up, there is no danger. [*A terrific flash of lightning and crash of thunder, a bolt descends and fires Jack's ship*]

NICK. The *Dolphin's* struck! Jack, your ship's on fire! [*Jack is panic-stricken. Clouds move on, rain descends in torrents in the distant horizon. Sun shines brighter than ever on shore. Margaret staggers to C.*]

MARG. [*With a superhuman effort*] Kneel my children. [*Jack and Mary kneel. Margaret raises hands aloft*] Father, we are in Thy hands, "Thy will be done."

(Chorus "Rock of Ages")

PICTURE AND END OF ACT

Percy
*

- - - -
- - - - -
- - - -
- - -

Margaret
* * * Hester

Jack Mary * Silas
*

ACT II.

TIME: *Fifteen months elapse. It is Christmas Eve. The interior of cabin represents an old ship's cabin; no plaster or whitewash, all oak timber with heads of wooden pegs, iron bolts, nuts, etc., seen. Good thickness of pieces on all doors and windows, borders represent roof or deck, everything very clean. Oblong window C. with white muslin curtain on drawing string, curtain drawn back so as to show distant sea and snow storm without. Oaken shutters outside windows to close and bar, oaken door L.U.E.; recess with curtains L.1.E. back by continuation of cabin bed with patch work quilt, in recess, arch with curtain. R.U.E. there is shown the continuation of cabin furnished; fireplace R.2.E. ship's locker against L. side of cabin, washstand with pitcher of water, bowl, soap, etc., etc., R.1.E., roller towel at stand, clothes rack, pegs, with southwestern coat, etc., R. of window, rubber boots beneath ship's glass on peg, old fashioned leaf table at window, dresser with dishes in R. arch, large photo of Jack, Mother and Mary over and at sides of window. Clock and ornaments on mantel, kettle steaming and singing on hob, cricket chirping on hearth. Within all warm and cozy, without storm howling; candles on mantel, lamp holly branches ready for Jack, dog and cat lying on hearth.*

MUSIC.

Sleigh bells heard ever and anon during scene. This carefully rehearsed. Low rocker for Mother, wooden chairs, flower stands with flowers R. and L.U. corners, small C. table, singing bird hanging in recess L., rag carpet, rugs, two oars, blades uppermost in corners behind flower stands. Snow to drift in at door and for characters, large watch, bundles, goose, etc., etc., for Jack, amber calciums R. and L. through window, red ditto through fireplace, fire log burning. Stage, semi-dark at rise to get effect of lights then gradually but imperceptibly light up, till full on, except borders behind window. Small mirror over washstand, beach and sea backing. 1st, act. drop.

DISCOVERED: *Margaret discovered in rocker knitting; Mary at table cutting out baby clothes; Jack at glass by washstand shaving; clean white shirt on bed in recess, stockings ready L.*

JACK. [*Washing his face and neck thoroughly in water and singing all the time, and drying himself on the towel. Sings "Oh! There was a jolly miller once, lived happy on the river Dee"*] There, that's over. Now Mary, where's my clean shirt?

MARY. There, Jack, on mother's bed, and your collar and handkerchief all ready.

JACK. Oh, Lord—Lord—what a little wife you are—eh mother! ain't she just the blessedest little wife in the world? [*Goes off L.1.*]

MARG. That she is, Jack, and you see that you prove the best of husbands to her.

JACK. [*Outside*] Oh! Never fear me—say, mother, don't you forget to hang up the stockings. Will ye?

MARY. [*Laughing*] Oh Jack! What nonsense!

JACK. [*Outside*] No nonsense about it; Christmas is Christmas! It comes but once a year—I'm goin' to have the stockings hung up—and I'm going to have lots of holly—and mince pie and goose and a regular New England jollification, there now: [*Coming out*] So, for fear you might forget it, I'll just hang them up myself. [*Comes out with stockings, one long black one, one long gray one, and one man's blue woolen sock*] Say, Mary hain't you got no better stocking than this? [*Shows black one*]

MARY. [*Going to him and trying to take the stockings from him*] Why, Jack, what ever are you going to do?

JACK. Hang up the stockings I tell you—[*She tries to get them; he puts them behind his back*] Now, it's no use little woman, ain't agoin' to give old Santa Claus any excuse. Ha! Ha! Ha! So, mother, you just give me some pins. [*Margaret feels in her breast, laughs, and gives him the pins. He puts them in his mouth*] Then Mother, first. [*Pins long gray one on line left of fire*] You next, Mary. [*Pins black one on line right of fire*] And me in the middle; there we be all in a row. [*Margaret has enjoyed this. Mary now comes down L. of stage, Jack stands C., admiring the stockings. Mary goes to him, she has baby's garment in her hand, places hand on his shoulder. Music*]

MARY. Jack, did you ever think that perhaps next Christmas there might be another stocking, a tiny one, Jack, to hang in the chimney corner?

JACK. Why, Mary child, there's tears in your eyes. [*Goes to wipe her eyes with the work she has, sees it's a baby's dress*] Why, bless my soul, what's this?

MARY. Do you remember Bella and John in *Our Mutual Friend*—that I read to you?

JACK. Yes, perfectly.

MARY. Well, there are sails Jack—sails for the little ship that's coming across the unknown sea—to you and me, Jack. [*Falls weeping in his arms. Margaret silently wipes her eyes. Jack is deeply affected, kisses Mary fervently. Silence and moment's pause*] Jack, have I been any comfort to you—have I made your life any happier by becoming your wife?

JACK. Happier! don't talk like that, Mary—why I couldn't live without you—now—

MARY. Then if anything should ever come between us—

JACK. Come between us—[*Fiercely*]

MARY. [*Placing hand over his mouth*] No! No! I don't mean that—I mean—if ever you should be tempted to—

JACK. [*Soothingly*] Oh! there I see now. [*Kisses her*] Bless you why didn't you say that before? There, I'll not go out at all—

MARY. [*Recovering herself*] Oh! yes, you must, your men expect you; it would be selfish of me to keep you here—don't mind me Jack—you know we women are apt to be moody and capricious when—

JACK. [*Stops her with a kiss*] Yes, yes, I know—I was only going because the men want to present me with a span new silver watch. Ho! Ho! Ho! and it says on it "to Jack Hepburne as a token of respect from his fellow workmen"—but I won't go.

MARY. [*Getting his coat*] Yes, yes—you must—there, now, see I'm all smiles again—now don't forget the holly—

JACK. [*Dressing*] No—nor the things for the stockings—nor the goose—mind, mother, that you put plenty of onions in the stuffin'—[*By this time he is dressed, kisses mother*] Good-bye. [*Kisses Mary*] I'll not be long away. [*Dog rises to follow*] No! No! Caesar, we mustn't both be absent at once; you stay here and take care of them till I come back, with my new silver watch. Mary you must keep asking me what time it is every hour in the day. Ho! Ho! Ho! [*Goes out; as he passes door, snow drifts in; Mary goes to window, as he passes, watches him, throws kiss, bursts into tears, rushes to Margaret and throws herself into her lap, weeping*]

MARG. Why, child alive—what's ever come over you? [*Smooths Mary's hair*]

MARY. I don't know, mother, it seems as if some great evil was about to fall upon us—try as I will I cannot shake it off. [*With fear*] Oh! Mother, if Jack should—

MARG. But he won't—you have been married now better than a good year —and has he not faithfully kept his promise?

MARY. [*Music changes; sleigh bells, etc.*] Yes.

MARG. Then trust him further, there dry your eyes—now and—[*Sleigh bells have become more distinct*]

SI. [*Outside*] Whoa, Deuteronomy! Whoa—boy! whoa! [*Bells stop*]

HES. [*Outside*] Help me out, Si Cummins, my legs is all twisted up in this horse blanket.

MARY. Hello! Visitors. [*Dries her eyes, looks through window and off L.*]

SI. Hold on till I hitch old Deuteronomy.

HES. Get me out I tell you—do you want me to freeze before I make my daybu?

SI. All right. All right. Gin us yer pump handles here—there ye are steady now. [*As they are heard approaching door, Mary goes to let them in. Silas stamps his feet and kicks his toes against door step. Mary opens door, snow drifts in; Silas enters carrying Hester. She is wrapped up in large old fashioned cloak and hood, heavy blue stockings over shoes; muffler on neck and mittens on hands; Silas in fur cap, long overcoat, with large white bone buttons, heavy boots, comforter around neck, mittens; they are covered in snow; he plumps Hester down before fire, starts to go off*]

MARY. Why, Silas, won't you warm yourself before you go?

SI. Oh!—Yes—I'll be back—I jist want to hitch Deuteronomy that's all.

MARY. Afraid he'll run away, Silas.

SI. Oh, no'm—afeard he'll fall down ef he hain't tied to suthin'. [*Goes off, all laugh*]

HES. [*Who has taken off her wraps, goes to Mrs. H.; kisses her*] Well, mother. [*Kisses Mary*] Merry Christmas.

MARY. [*Smiling*] Aren't you a little early?

HES. Well, you see I shan't have time tomorrow—I'll be awful busy tomorrow. Have you seen the bills?

MARY. Bills! What bills?

HES. The play bills, of course—what other bills are there? Lampey's—you know he's here for the holidays. [*Silas enters, shakes snow off coat, cap, and feet; takes off great coat, comforter, cap and mittens, lays them on locker*]

MARY. Yes—I know that—we are all going—Jack is to take us tomorrow night.

HES. [*Clapping her hands*] Is he—ah—good—ain't that splendid—got your seats?

MARY. I don't know, I presume so, however.

HES. If you ain't you better get 'em, there'll be a jam.

SI. Ye kin get 'em at my store—got a few choice reserves at five cents extra.

HES. Do you think ye'll know me?

MARY. Know you!

HES. Yes—I'm going to make my *day*-bu—

SI. An so'mi—

MARY. [*In surprise, but with a pleased expression*] What?

HES. Yes—Lampey says he will waive patronage—and try talent.

SI. Yes—he's gin us a chance—though he says he don't think talent's much yuse.

MARY. Well—I'm sure I'm *de*lighted—tomorrow evening—eh!

HES. [*Grandiloquently*] Tomorrow evening. [*Waves her hand*]

SI. I lead the band waggin twicet—morning and afternoon—but Hester stars in the evening.

HES. Show her the bill, Silas.

SI. I will. [*Gets out play bill*]

MARY. [*Takes it, reads*] Town Hall, Gloucester, extraordinary attraction. Engagement at enormous expense of the young, beautiful and talented comedienne, Miss Hester Barton, assisted by the incomparable musician and pharmacoepeist, Mr. Silas Cummings, who will appear for one night only, Thursday, Dec. 25th, in conjunction with Lampey's Dramatic Constellation in a monster programme. Secure your seats at Cumming's drug store and avoid the rush at the doors. N.B. weather permitting band chariot, drawn by six snow white Arabian steeds will parade the principal streets at nine A.M. and one P.M.

SI. The band's chariot's Aleck Pearce's ice cart with flags over it.

HES. S—I—L—A—S—

MARY. And Silas Cummings will lead Lampey's Metropolitan Band of forty pieces and perform several popular solos on the clarionet. Well—well—that is splendid—but why do you only play one night?

SI. Lampey thinks one night's enuff.

MARY. But the bill don't say what you do, what do you do?

SI. Lampey'll announce that from the stage. I think it's safest.

MARY. Safest? In what way?

SI. Cos ef any eggs is fired, Lampey'll git 'em.

HES. Oh! Silas ain't you awful? Why Mary, I sing a ballad and for an encore Silas and me do a double song and dance.

SI. Say—s'pose there hain't no encore.

HES. Oh, there's sure to be—we rehearsed it this morning and Lampey said it would paralyze 'em.

SI. Or they'll paralyze us.

HES. Would you like to hear us rehearse?

MARY. Should be delighted.

HES. Come along Silas. [*Getting ready to sing and dance*] Mary'll play for us. [*Gives roll of music; Mary goes to piano*]

SI. I hain't thawed 'eout yet.

HES. You just come along—you mean thing. [*Pulls him up*]

SI. I got a corn on my heel.

HES. Ready, Mary.

MARY. All ready?

SI. Let 'er go, Gallagher. [*Song and dance*]

MARY. Bravo—Bravo—why Silas you're quite an actor. [*It has grown quite dark outside by this*]

HES. Oh, he's got to act if he wants to marry me—I'll never marry anyone but an actor. [*Silas and Hester get ready to go*]

SI. Oh! I'll act—I'll act—only let the audience keep their claws off—an' I'll act.

MARY. Won't you stay to tea—Jack'll be back soon—he'd like you to stay to tea, I know.

HES. No, thank you—I've got my wardrobe to look after and my *theatre trunk*, ahem! to pack.

SI. Yes—an' I've got to give Deuteronomy a coat of whitewash and git him ready for one of the six snow white Arabian steeds. [*By this time they're ready to go*] So I guess we'd best be off—goodnight.

HES. [*Kissing Margaret and Mary*] Good night and a happy Christmas to you, as for me this'll be the happiest Christmas of my life—be sure you come early—so as not to miss any of me—and get good seats—good night—[*Talking as she goes off*]

MARY. Good night. [*They are off now*]

SI. Whoa,—Deuteronomy—[*Sleigh bells tinkle as Silas removes blanket and gets into sleigh, and chirks merrily as they ride off. Mary watches them through the window till they disappear, kissing hand to them, then lights candles and lamp, opens window, as it is now quite dark, closes shutters, draws curtain*]

MARY. [*As she works*] Ah! dear, light hearted little Hester—I hope her début will be a success, I'm sure—it will break her heart to fail—I must ask Jack to get me some flowers to throw to her.

MARG. Well—for my part, I never set much store by play actors—though they may be as good as any one else for all I know.

MARY. Yes, mother, there are good and bad in all lines of life—the player I presume is no exception to the rule. [*She now wheels the C. table away, the big table C. and prepares to set the supper table*] Hark! I thought that was Jack's step—[*Laughs*] Poor fellow, how proud he'll be of his watch and how like a great boy he insisted on hanging the stockings. [*Kettle begins to sing*] Why, even the kettle is merry tonight. [*Cricket chirps*] And the cricket, too, bless me, quite a happy family, come puss—[*To cat*] haven't you a note to add to the chorus and you Caesar—[*To dog*] Come sir, get ready to welcome your master. [*By this time she has finished the table*] There we are all ready now, I'll just put the tea to draw—[*Does so*] Now for Jack's favorite preserves—[*Goes into recess R., brings cake dish with cake in it and glass dish of preserves—Christmas carol heard in the distance—she stops and listens—it grows gradually nearer—passes window*] Hark! Mother! Is not that sweet—Ah! blessed, happy—happy Christmas—[*Resumes work—brings meat and bread from dresser—cuts bread, etc., etc., Christmas carol dies gradually away —and "we won't go home till morning" begins in the distance—she stops—listens—staggers—leans on table—singing comes nearer—nearer—ends near door. There is a loud laugh—door bursts open—Jack staggers in very drunk —laden with bundles. He wears a watch and has holly branches and wreathes. He drops them all on floor, staggers to locker, falls full length on it in drunken stupor—Mary shrieks—and falls senseless on floor. Margaret rises, falls on knees in prayer. Percy appears at door in handsome winter suit, snow drifts in through door—wind howls—sleigh bells in distance, chorus outside "Rock of Ages."*

PICTURE AND END OF ACT

ACT III.

SCENE I: *The City. Night. Five years have elapsed. Residence of the Seward's. A grand hop in preparation. Carpets down all through covered with drugget; everything very elegant. Flowers, statuary, chandeliers, side lights, etc., etc.*

Magnificent garden illuminated by electricity. Balustrade of second story balcony overlooking garden.

Music.

At rise, as curtain ascends, male servant in livery, descends staircase carrying a large vase of flowers. This servant a tall, fat man, very particular for business with Silas at end of Act. Crosses to folding doors R., enters apartment, exits, after a moment's elapse returns without flowers, crosses and exits C. and L. At same time female servant with cap, apron, collar, cuffs, etc., etc., dressed in new stiff dress, supposed to be her best, enters from R.H. arch and crosses to apartment L.1.E. and exits passing male servant in livery who enters R.1.E., and exits up staircase as the female servants enter from R.C. and exits up staircase. These four servants stand ready for Act, to cross and re-cross as directed at rehearsal. There is music in the garden and laughter before and after curtain till the scene is well begun. Enter down staircase Mrs. Seward, a dark, dignified lady, with a stern but just face, elegantly and quietly dressed, and Mary, elegantly attired but wearing a saddened expression of face.

Mrs. S. [*Leading Mary to tête a tête R. and seating her*] There my child, for you are now my child. My son has told me your story and although I am proud, and at first strongly opposed him in what I believed a mad infatuation, yet I could not permit my pride to stand as a barrier to his happiness. He—loves—you—you are his wife and I love you too. Percy tells me that your first husband has been dead four years.

Mary. Dead four years! [*Aside*]—to me. To me. [*Aloud*] Yes madam.

Mrs. S. Do not call me madam, call me mother.

Mary. [*Looks at her wistfully, hesitates, then suddenly falls on her knees, her head in Mrs. Seward's lap*] Mother! [*She bursts into tears as Percy enters C.L.*]

Mrs. S. [*Kissing her*] That's right—[*Smooths Mary's hair in the way Jack's mother did in Act II*] That's right, I must leave you now and show myself among your guests. [*Sees Percy*] Ah! my son, you come very apropos. Mary seems a little sad and downhearted, cheer her up—you can—for who can comfort and cheer a young wife like her young husband? [*Smiles very kindly yet with quiet dignity and exits C.L. At the word wife Percy seems a little embarrassed, slightly drops his head, not enough to be noticed by Mrs. Seward. As his mother goes, he crosses to Mary*]

Percy. Why Mary darling, do not give way like this.

MARY. Percy, is this right?

PERCY. Is what right?

MARY. This deceit—this living lie—Oh! Percy I have never deceived a human being before. And to think that the first should be the one to whom you owe so much—your noble mother—Percy—think—she bade me call her *Mother*—and that sacred name—that I have so yearned—so *hungered* for—I uttered tonight with a lie in my heart—Shame! shame!! shame! [*Crosses L. and flings herself in chair*]

PERCY. You look only on the blackness of the clouds; you will not see the silver lining beyond.

MARY. Ah! Percy, I fear there is no silver lining for me.

PERCY. [*Continuing*] Besides—you are my wife in the sight of Heaven, you will soon be so in the face of man.

MARY. Yes, Percy! I believe you honestly intend all you say, and that you will, if permitted, perform all that you have promised, but the fact remains, that until that time I am but your—

PERCY. [*Alarmed*] Hush, my darling, hush!

MARY. Percy, have you never been haunted by the thought that *he* might still live?

PERCY. [*Decidedly*] Never! I tell you his death is almost certain. Four years and no word or sign from him. Four years since his ship was lost and never a soul left to tell the tale. There! There! Wait but the return of my messenger with the confirmation he is certain to bring, [*Cheerfully*] then for a quiet little marriage and I trust a long and happy life. [*Laughter outside L.C.*] Ah! Here are your eccentric friends, it will go hard if they do not bring the smiles back to your lips—I verily believe Miss Barton would chase away a fit of the blue imps itself. Ha! Ha! [*Exit through folding door R. At the same time enter C., from L., Hester, handsomely attired in what is supposed to be a stage dress, with a very long train, which is carried by Silas. He is in full evening dress, with very tight pantaloons. As Hester sees Mary, she makes a rush towards her. Silas, not starting quickly enough, almost falls, and the train comes off in his hands. Picture. Hester's dress is made so that it is complete even without the train, she does not know that it is off, but goes directly to Mary. Silas stands dismayed, looks at Hester, then at dress, tries to speak, his tongue cleaves to roof of his mouth. Keeps this business up just a moment. He must not over do this,—points to Hester, then to dress, then to himself in despair. A happy thought strikes him, he hastily folds up train, just then servant maid enters, down staircase, and crosses to R.C. He sees her, taps her on shoulder and presents her with train. She accepts, curtseys very low, he kisses her, she is pleased; curtseys again, he bows, she exits. He comes down left, very highly pleased with himself as much as to say "I flatter myself that was decidedly neat." Meantime Hester has gone to Mary, shaken both hands, kissed her, and talks all through Silas' business*]

HES. Oh Mary! Ahem! I beg pardon, Mrs. Seward. [*Mary checks her*] Let me look at you. Well I declare if you ain't just beautiful—you look for all the world as if you were born here and had lived here all your life, and had never been within a thousand miles of old Gloucester.

MARY. Dear Old Gloucester, I fear I was happier there than I ever shall be here.

HES. Oh! How can you say so. For my part I hate the very name of the place. Paugh! I can smell it now.

SI. Kin ye? Well then ye've got a derned sight better smellin' factory than I hev, and I'm willin' to at that—I'd give suthin to jest poke my *oil* factory into Old Heminway's packin' shed this minit. [*Snuffs*] I jest love the smell o' fish.

HES. I dare say,—you'd rather be stuck behind that dilapidated pill counter of yours, peddling blood root than gratifying a lofty ambition.

SI. Lofty ambition be blowed! Blood root is better than actin' enny day—blood root's ghost allus walks; that's one thing.

HES. Silas, that's a cowardly allusion to poor Mr. Lampey's misfortunes.

SI. I wish Mr. Lampey'd drink less and pay more salaries.

HES. [*To Mary*] You must know my dear that I'm Lampey's stock star now, and *such* a favorite. I have a carriage to and from—stop at all the best hotels.

SI. She don't know that I have to peddle appetite pills and corn salve on the Q.T. to pay the bills.

HES. And I *have* an *understudy*—and Silas, he's Juvenile Tragedy and leads the orchestra.

SI. [*Aside*] Orchestra! Clarionette and one fiddle.

HES. You just ought to see Silas play "Alonzo the Brave." Oh! my, but he is splendid and then at the end, in the great scene where he takes the poison, he crawls off L.H., in dying agony and plays the slow music to let the curtain down; he's great—Lampey says he's a better actor than Booth.

SI. I guess I am, but Booth gets more pay.

HES. Just play that poison scene for her Silas.

SI. I hain't got no pizen—'sides ef I fell deown in these ere pants, [*With significance*] I'd—well—ye'd have to ring deown that's all—

HES. Well then give a recitation.

SI. I hain't no good recitator.

HES. You are, too.

SI. [*Yielding, wanting to be urged*] I *can't act.*

HES. You can too.

SI. I tell ye I can't.

HES. You can, too.

SI. Well I'll give you a recitation. [NOTE: *This must be delivered in dead earnest, with no attempt at burlesque except what the natural twang and character of the man gives it. Silas really thinks he's great*]

MARY and HES. [*Clapping hands*] Bravo! Bravo!

HES. Ain't he just splendid? I wish Mr. Field could hear him—he'd soon have Barron's place. Mary, why don't you go on the stage; Lampey could advertise you so now; you've got such notes. [*Sees that Mary is pained, checks herself*] No, I didn't mean that. [*Hastily changes the subject*] How do you like my dress?

MARY. It's beautiful, I'm sure.

HES. Hain't too good, is it? [*Whispers*] It's one of my stage dresses—[*Laughs*] how do you like my train? [*Turning around*] Is it too long?

SI. Ahem! [*Begins to hum to himself and turns up stage*]

MARY. [*Not knowing anything about the train, thinking Hester joking, smiles*] Ah! no! I should say not a bit too long.

SI. [*Reassured*] No, I should say just about the right *lenth.*

HES. But when is the dancing to begin! I love to dance.

MARY. [*Kissing her*] Hester dear, I believe you were born dancing and will leave this world singing your way into the next. [*Takes Hester's face between her hands and looks earnestly at her*] If there were only more like you, the world would be better for it; you are a ray of sunshine to me, so sing and dance to your heart's content: You merry—harmless—hopeful little cricket. [*Kisses her and exits R.*]

HES. [*Who has been affected, looks after her, bursts into tears, crosses, throws herself on Silas' breast*] W-h-a-a-t—d-i-d—she—make me cry for?

SI. [*Wiping his eyes, in a hoarse whisper*] I don't know.

HES. [*Drying her eyes*] I think it was real mean of her: Just as I wanted to look nice. Is my nose red?

SI. No, is mine?

HES. No—wait—[*Takes powder, rag and small glass out of pocket, powders Silas' nose, then her own*] There now we are all right, let's go and find the company. [*Starts to go; waltz heard behind scenes; she stops*] Ah Silas, my waltz song. [*She listens, tries to restrain herself, but can't; gracefully begins to waltz and hum to herself. Silas does the same, and finally she seizes Silas and whirls him away in waltz. Waltz, song and dance by*

Silas and Hester. NOTE: *Very neat at the end, all the Guests waltz on through C. arches R.L.* NOTE: *If encore, guests waltz at back but do not sing. Hester utterly absorbed sees nothing—knows nothing. Mary enters R.H. takes her from Silas and they waltz off R. Waltz continued outside, Silas waltzes by himself. Miss Stanley enters R.C. from R., he waltzes against her*]

SI. Beg pardin'.

MISS S. Are you waiter here?

SI. Yes, been waitin' some time for the dancin' to begin.

MISS S. I don't mean that. How long have you been tender here. [*Inadvertently placing her hand over her heart*]

SI. [*Same business*] *Tender* here, wa'al I hain't been here long, but if you stand there looking at me that 'ere way—there's no knowing how tender I may git.

MISS S. Oh pshaw! I mean are you a hired domestic.

SI. *Me! No!* I'm one o' the company.

MISS S. I beg your pardon. [*Curtseys very low*]

SI. Don't mention it. [*Curtseys very absurdly*]

MISS S. I—dear me—how awkward—I—hope, [*Curtsying and getting toward C.R.*] You'll excuse—[*Exits, he following to entrance bowing and assuring her that there is no harm done; enter from C.L. Miss Fairchild, fanning herself, throws herself on ottoman L. quite exhausted*]

MISS F. Here—you! [*Silas, bowing after Miss S.*] Young man! [*He turns*]

SI. Mean me, Miss?

MISS F. Yes, get me a lemonade.

SI. Where'll I get it?

MISS F. On the sideboard there. Stupid! [*Points to R. arch*]

SI. In there?

MISS F. Yes—yes—be quick please.

SI. All right. [*Goes off, Miss Fairchild lies back and fans herself. Silas re-enters with lemonade with a straw in it*] Here ye are, Miss.

MISS F. Is it sweet?

SI. I guess so. [*Sucks through straw*] Yes, it's very sweet. [*Offers it*]

MISS F. You insolent—how dare—you—[*About to flounce off C.R., Silas following with lemonade*]

SI. Here's yer lemonade, don't you want it?

MISS F. I'll have you discharged for this. [*Exits very angry, C.R.*]

SI. Discharged! Goin' to tell Lampey on me, I don't care—this lemonade's all fired good though. [*Drinks it, places glass on stand L. Enter Miss Easter-*

brook C. from R. with wrap as if from garden; throws off wrap as she enters, sees Silas]

MISS E. Here young man, take this to the ladies' dressing room. [*Exits C.L.*]

SI. Ladies' dressin' room! [*Looks around, laughs*] Gosh! They won't let me into the Ladies' dressin' room. [*Same maid to whom he gave train now enters R. arch. Silas stops her, presents wrap;—same business as with train. She exits up staircase*] That's the second present I've gin that gal this evening, if I keep on she'll hev a regular Christmas. [*Enter all the guests R. and L.*]

HARRY. Now then, partners and places for a quadrille.

SI. [*Calling him*] Mr.—[*Touching him on shoulder*] Mr.—

HARRY. Merton, Sir.

SI. Merton sir—will you please to introduce me to a partner.

HARRY. Certainly, your name?

SI. Cummins. Silas Cummins. [*During this time Miss Stanley, Miss Fairchild and Miss Easterbrook have been in the foreground, whispering and pointing to Silas. Miss Stanley is telling them that he is a guest; they laugh, blush, etc. Harry goes up to Miss Easterbrook, speaks to her, she assents, brings her down, etc., introduces her to Silas*]

HARRY. Mr. Cummings, Miss Easterbrook. [*They bow, etc. Silas very awkwardly*]

SI. [*Aside*] That's the gal that gin me the shawl.

MISS E. Mr. Cummings, I believe I owe you an apology.

SI. Don't mention it. [*Aside*] I owe her a shawl.

HARRY. All ready? [*Dance. This must be arranged to give Silas all the opportunity for fun; he must be careful not to exceed the bounds of propriety; at one portion of the dance, and at its end, Silas does some terrific leaps and steps; stops suddenly, all stop in amazement, he sides over to R.H.1E.*] What's the matter?

SI. Nothin' only you'll hev to excuse me, jist get some one else to take my place a minit. Will ye? [*At this a tall fat servant enters from L.1. Crosses to R.1E. Silas seizes him, whispers in his ear. He laughs and assents and exits R.1. as Silas sides off, keeping face towards company*] I knowed them blame trousers was too tight when I put 'em on. [*Exit R.1E. at same time servant enters R. arch*]

SERVANT. Supper. [*Music changes to march, all exit R.H. Music changes. Enter Jack L.C. gray hair, pale, aged, ill, but with an endeavor to present a cleanly appearance. He is clad in a sailor suit, very poor. At same time enter from R.1E. Mary and Hester. Mary now quite cheerful as through the influence of Hester*]

HES. [*Speaking as she enters*] My dear Mary what an elegant place you have here, to be sure; next to being on the stage, I know of nothing that would please me so well as living like this.

MARY. Ah, Hester dear, you must remember the old saw "All is not gold that glitters." [*By this time they have gotten quite close to Jack who has been staring at them. Mary, who has been looking squarely into Hester's face, and Hester into hers, now looks up and meets Jack's eyes*] Jack! [*Hester astonished, shrinks as if afraid*]

JACK. Yes.

MARY. [*Much moved*] We—[*Corrects herself*] I thought you dead.

JACK. The boon of death is not given to men like me.

MARY. Hester—run—keep—him—[*Corrects herself*] *Them* from coming here. [*Hester runs off R. arch*] What has brought you here?

JACK. To see you.

MARY. You have grown strangely considerate, after four years of silent absence.

JACK. After that fatal night four years ago—the night—that in my delirium—I—so far forgot myself as to—

MARY. [*As if ashamed to revert to it*] Hush!

JACK. Oh! Why was not my arm palsied first? I fled the cabin—and sought my refuge—the dram shop—I knew no more till I found myself at my old trade—bound on a fishing cruise aboard the "Sprite."

MARY. All this I know.

JACK. The "Sprite" was wrecked, as you must also know. All on board—save myself—went down. After sixty hours I was picked up by an outward bound brig—a trader in the China Seas. For weeks I lay between life and death—at last we were overhauled by a Chinese Pirate and I doomed to a living death—service aboard her. I escaped and I know not how I reached the old—old place; reached it to find the cabin ashes—you gone. To my inquiries I could only learn that you were in the city. I came here—watched—searched high and low—at last I bethought me of Mr. Seward and that possibly he could aid me—I inquired of a policeman where he could be found, "Why," said he, "there is his carriage now"—I looked, and in it saw you. You know the rest—they tell me you are—

MARY. [*Firmly, but not tauntingly*] I *am*—and who has made me what I am? [*He hangs his head*] Jack Hepburne—I loved you from the first hour in which I learned to lisp your name—I clambered upon your knees in childhood—walked hand in hand with you to church in girlhood, in maidenhood, watched, with tear dimmed eyes, each departing vessel as it bore you from me, and every night upon my knees sent forth the orphan's prayer to the

God of the fatherless for your speedy and safe return. At last what had been a seed—a blade—a leaf—a bud burst forth in blossom—and became a peerless flower—a priceless gem—a *woman's* pure and holy love—and *still* 'twas all your own—what did you with it? [NOTE: *this speech with all the firm decisive pathos possible, quiet but intensely strong*]

JACK. I know—I know—

MARY. [*Continuing*] After one year of bliss, the like of which my yearning soul never even pictured to itself—you forgot your promises—forgot your oath—cast aside my love and *became* a drunkard.

JACK. [*Groaning in shame*] Oh! My God! my God—

MARY. For still another year I bore it—I hoped against hope—I strove by every means in human power to save you—to reclaim you—to bring you back to manhood—and to self—in vain. Where I looked for loving words—I found neglect—where I sought happiness, I found poverty and despair. At last with my arms clasped fast about your neck in woman's weak endeavor to shield you from your demon—you struck me to your feet and fled—I who had loved you so—who became your wife—the mother of your child—

JACK. Enough! enough!

MARY. And now you seek me for what, to drag me back to the old life? *Never.* But do not think it is this luxury that binds me here—I would rather share one humble crust with Jack Hepburne than all the wealth a king could offer—but Jack Hepburne—*my* Jack Hepburne is dead—and I will not accept this semblance that has risen in his stead.

JACK. You wrong me, Mary—I do not come to ask you to share my lot—I have none to offer. The hospital and when strong enough, the sea is my only refuge now—I will not take from you the life within your grasp.

MARY. [*Struggling with her tears*] Ah! If you only knew.

JACK. But tell me, Mary, our child—our little Margaret—is she alive?

MARY. Yes.

JACK. [*Wiping eyes*] And well?

MARY. And well.

JACK. [*Almost afraid to ask*] Is—is—she here?

MARY. She is safe. Know that it is for her sake and hers alone that I am here—I would not have her meet my sad fate—and—so—[*Slowly almost vacantly*] I sold the mother to save the child.

JACK. [*With bowed head*] May—I—see her?

MARY. [*Looks at him almost as if she would go to him at this tearful request. He does not see the action, after an effort*] It is better not—the image of the father I have taught her to pray for night and morning is sacredly engraven on her young heart—best not destroy it—

JACK. Be it so—mother is I suppose—

MARY. Dead! Yes—her last thoughts were of you: Her last words "Jack!—poor Jack."

JACK. [*Raises his eyes to Heaven as if he saw her*] Mother! [*Breathes a silent prayer*] Well I will go now. Farewell.

MARY. [*Much moved*] Is there nothing I can do for you? Do you not need money?

JACK. [*Looks at her reproachfully*] Ah! Mary—not that—spare me that—no—not *his* money—[*Jack is going, Mary makes motion as if impelled to follow or stay him. At same time enter Mrs. Seward, Percy, R. and Hester backing on trying to stay them*]

HES. But I tell you, madam, she is not quite ready yet; I assure you I will bring her, I beg of you to return to the guests.

MRS. S. Nonsense child, I will know what detains my daughter; when courtesy demands her presence amongst her guests. [*Sees Jack*] *Mercy on us, what is this!*

PERCY. [*Aside startled*] He here!

HES. Now for the fifth act.

Mrs. S.

Percy

Hester Jack

Mary

R. L.

MRS. S. [*Sees the picture of alarm on all faces and suspects something wrong*] Who are you, sir? [*To Jack*]

JACK. A shipwrecked sailor.

MRS. S. What seek you here?

JACK. [*With meaning*] Charity!

MRS. S. Do you know this woman? [*Points to Mary*]

PERCY. Mother!

MRS. S. Silence! [*Repeating question*] Do you know this woman?

JACK. [*Raises head slowly, looks at Mary, deep struggle*] No. [*Percy breathes a long breath of relief. Mary makes no movement*]

MRS. S. Then leave this apartment—go below; the servants will see that your wants are met. How dare you intrude your presence here? [*Jack bows, silently turns to go, at same time little Margaret runs on from first entrance L. with doll, and runs directly to Mary*]

LITTLE M. Oh! Mama! See what a beautiful dress Louise has made for my doll. [*At the sound of her voice Jack stops at the word "mama." Unable to restrain himself he shrieks*]

JACK. *My child!* [*Checks himself, but sees it is too late. He is dazed. A picture of dismay on all faces, except Mary's, who has made no movement during scene; and Mrs. Seward's, who wears the expression of wounded pride*]

MRS. S. His child. Percy what is the meaning of this? [*All the guests quietly enter from R. Silas with large pantaloons enters R.1. Hester goes down to him, she is explaining in dumb show*]

PERCY. I cannot answer.

MRS. S. [*To Mary*] Speak you, madam, who is this man?

MARY. [*Calmly*] My husband.

MRS. S. [*To Percy*] And you have dared to insult me thus—

PERCY. Mother, hear me.

MRS. S. Silence! As for you madam—I—pity you—but—leave—my house —go—[*Mary makes no motion, slowly crosses, leading her child; she offers her hand, Jack takes it in act of moving off, Hester and Silas following*]

Guests Servants

Percy Mrs. S.

Mary Jack

Silas Little Margaret

ACT IV.

SCENE 1: *Garret in North End, very squalid; bed, wooden table and one chair, old stove in fireplace, no fire; door L., boxing attic window R.F., candle in old candlestick lighted on table. Backing, a dirty hall in tenement house.*

window

table door

stove

chair

bed

Little Margaret discovered in bed, Mary kneeling beside her. Mary is very poorly dressed, pale and thin. Jack enters slowly and despondently. Mary who has been intently listening to baby's breathing hears him, and motions to him to make no noise. He enters on tip-toe; he is very pale and haggard.

MARY. Hush! Step lightly, she is asleep. Well! [*Spoken in hoarse whisper*]

JACK. [*Despairingly, shaking head*] Nothing, no work, no bread.

MARY. Did you go to him?

JACK. Yes: Even to him. His mother has sent him abroad; she is pitiless. How is baby?

MARY. Worse Jack, I fear she is starving.

JACK. Starving! No! No! Not that, [*wild*] it cannot be—it shall not be—by God! I'll tear food from their—

MARY. [*Staying him*] Hush.

LITTLE M. [*Faintly*] Mama!

MARY. [*Goes quickly to her*] Yes, my darling.

LITTLE M. I'm *so* hungry. Are you hungry, mama?

MARY. [*Almost choking, Jack stands, wild*] No, my darling.

LITTLE M. It's dreadful to be hungry, ain't it, mama?

MARY [*Rushing to Jack, hoarsely but furiously*] Do you hear, Jack? Go, beg, steal, *murder,* but bring food to my starving child.

JACK. [*Desperately*] I will. [*Rushes out*]

LITTLE M. Mama. [*Mary goes to her*]

MARY. My baby.

LITTLE M. Is papa gone?

MARY. Yes dear, he has gone to get bread for my baby.

LITTLE M. Will he come back soon?

MARY. Yes dear, very soon.

LITTLE M. Oh! mama, I had such a beautiful dream.

MARY. Did you dear?

LITTLE M. Would you like to hear it?

MARY. Yes darling, tell mama your little dream.

LITTLE M. I dreamed that papa had never gone away, that we were all back in our own beautiful home; not that great big home, but our own little home by the bright, blue sea.

MARY. Yes, dear.

LITTLE M. And gran'ma was there, not that grand gran'ma, but my own beautiful gran'ma; and we were all *so* happy, and we went down to the sea and watched the ships sailing up and down, and they looked like great, white birds floating on the water.

MARY. Yes, dear.

LITTLE M. And the sea was so still and bright, and the sun so shiny and warm, and the sky was so blue; and pretty soon there came a great black cloud, and the sun went *out.*

MARY. My baby!

LITTLE M. And the sea began to roar, and the big waves threw the poor ships clear away up to the sky almost. And ah! such a dreadful storm as I never saw before.

MARY. Was my baby frightened?

LITTLE M. Ah! Yes mama, so frightened.

MARY. It was only a dream, my darling.

LITTLE M. I know mama, but it frightened me all the same, but the storm didn't stay long.

MARY. Didn't it, dear?

LITTLE M. No mama, it went away, and the sea got still again, and pretty soon I looked up and I saw such a beautiful ship, all gold and silver, coming right to us, and it came and took you and papa and gran'ma and me and dolly, and sailed away to the most beautiful land. It seemed like the fairy land you used to read to me about, and ah! mama, look! [*Raising up in bed; Mary holds her*] The ship—call papa—quick.

MARY. There is no ship darling, you are dreaming still.

LITTLE M. No mama, there—don't you see? Look! the angels, sailing over it, they're calling us mama. Come! [*She gets up in bed. Mary holds her and tries to calm her*]

MARY. There, there, my child, lie down. [*Almost frantic, she realizes that death has come, but dare not give way*]

LITTLE M. Don't you hear mama? They are calling you too. Come mama, or the beautiful ship will be gone. Quick! [*Makes a step*] Ah mama, [*Crying*] give me your hand, it's all dark now; I can't see the ship, it's all dark. Where are you, mama?

MARY. [*Holding her in her arms*] Here darling, here.

LITTLE M. Kiss me, mama. I wish papa would come, will he know that the ship took you and me? There it is again, I'm coming, I—goodbye papa, come mama, come! see! I—[*She dies. Mary lays her down, closes her eyes, takes her hand and hides her own head in the bed clothes. The door bursts open. Jack enters, followed by Hester and Silas, he is laden with food*]

JACK. See! Mary! *food! food!* at last.

MARY. Too late, Jack, she's dead. [*Jack drops food, stands transfixed, Hester and Silas get around to R. of bed*]

HES. Mary—see—we've found you at last.

MARY. Oh! Hester—she's gone—my beautiful baby, my little Margaret's gone—see—isn't she beautiful? See the smile upon her lips—she is waiting for me—she wants her mother. Yes—baby—I'll come to you—Jack—[*Half turning to Jack*]—I love you Jack—I forgive and love you—but I cannot stay —I must go with baby—don't blame me—and don't mourn, it was to be.

You remember the storm on our wedding day—well it has ended at last—don't drink Jack! Be brave—be my old, old Jack once more. Goodbye, Hester, dear kind Hester and Silas too. Ah Silas! I'll never ride Deuteronomy again. [*As if to baby*] Yes, yes I'm coming, good—bye—I'm coming. [*She turns and quietly dies, with her back against the bed and her head on the child's body*]

HES. Jack—Jack—she's dead!

JACK. [*Who has not moved, stares wildly around and sees Mary's body and goes to her*] Why Mary girl, what is the matter with you, child? Oh I see—well—well—I'll not go out tonight; let the watch go. Come let's fill the stockin's, perhaps in a year there may be another stockin' hangin' here. Ha! ha! ha! there Caesar, you stop here with them—Mary be sure you keep askin' me the time o' day. Ha! ha! ha! Why, what place is this? I won't stay here, come Mary, let's go. [*He lifts her and supports her in his arms; her dead body is limp, but he is strong*] Let's go home, back to the old home in Gloucester—[*Kisses her*] Poor child—I have so loved—so wronged you. But I'll make amends—I'll drink no more, come. Mother, be sure you put plenty of onions in the stuffin'—Mother—see—here's Mary—she's not well, poor girl—quick, food. She's starvin', I tell you—come Mary, we'll go home—home—home—[*Moving towards door with dead body of Mary, Hester and Silas horrified but unable to stay him*]

PICTURE AND CURTAIN

ACT V.

SCENE: *Christmas Morning.*
MUSIC: *Same as Act II—early morning, the table cleared away, the shutters open and the sun streaming in. Holly wreaths hanging on each end of mother's picture, one on Mary's, one on Jack's: Holly branches over window and mantel; stockings filled. Mother discovered knitting by fire, Mary cutting dress, dog and cat on hearth; Jack asleep, as he had fallen. Sleigh bells heard in distance before curtain goes up and all through scene. Music kept up till Jack's scene well on.*

JACK. [*In his sleep*] No—no—you shall not tear her away from me—I tell you she is not dead—let her go—[*Furiously*] I tell you let her go—I—do you hear? [*Springs up*] Let her go. [*Mary has stopped work at his first ravings and comes down L. as he gets C.*] Let her go—I'll brain the first man who—[*He sees Mary, then Margaret, then mother*] Mary, mother—[*With a wild cry*] A dream! Thank God! A dream! [*Falls sobbing hysterically at his mother's knees*]

MARY. Why Jack, what ever has come over you?

JACK. [*Jumps up, takes her to his breast*] Ah! Mary, Mary, I've had such a horrid dream—but you're not dead, [*Almost smothering her with kisses*] and mother's not dead—and the bab—

MARY. Hush Jack, all in good time, Heaven willing. [*Taking off Jack's heavy coat, hanging it up. Christmas carol in distance*]

JACK. [*Catching her as she comes down and kissing her*] But you're sure you're not dead, Mary?

MARY. [*Smiling*] Quite sure Jack.

JACK. And mother—bless her dear old face. Are you quite sure you're not dead, mother?

MARG. I'm worth a dozen dead women yet, Jack. [*Jack kisses her*]

JACK. Ah Mary! I have had such a dream, but it's a lesson to me. [*Seriously*] Mary! will you trust poor Jack once more?

MARY. With all my heart—I trust you as I love you Jack.

JACK. [*Seriously*] I'll never break my word again—I swear it on the "Rock of Ages." [*Christmas carol has come nearer and nearer, finishes now; and Hester, Silas and fishermen and village girls all in holiday attire burst in with—*]

OMNES. Merry Christmas! Merry Christmas.

JACK. Merry Christmas! Merry Christmas.

MARY. Merry Christmas! Merry Christmas!

MARG. Merry Christmas! [*Mary and Hester kiss, Hester kisses Margaret. Silas goes down L. and shakes hands with Jack*] What time is it Jack?

JACK. Ah Silas! I've had such a dreadful dream.

SI. Hev ye, a few appetite pills or a little blood root'll cure them. [*Sleigh bells very heavy have approached door. The driver says "whoa!" Noise of stopping sleigh; enter Percy well wrapped and all smiles*]

PERCY. Merry Christmas to you all.

MARY. Thank you, Mr. Seward, the same to you and many of them. [*Silas goes up, Percy comes down, at the sound of his voice Jack starts as if he could not realize*]

PERCY. [*Giving hand*] Merry Christmas, Mr. Hepburne.

JACK. [*Sternly*] The last time I see you—you was—[*Checks himself, grasps hand heartily*] A thousand of 'em, sir, and there ain't no man that I'm gladder to see here this day than you.

PERCY. Thank you, and now my friends I have a proposition to make—I have outside a sleigh and six prancing horses—

SI. I hope they hain't Lampey's six snow white Arabians.

PERCY. The sleigh will just hold this party, so I invite you all to a jolly sleigh ride, a good old fashioned Christmas dinner, and a visit to Lampey's to do honor to our fair debutante and finish up the festivities in the evening. What say you?

ALL. Yes, yes, three cheers for Mr. Seward, the Fisherman's Santa Claus. Huzza—huzza—huzza—

PERCY. And long life and happiness to Jack Hepburne and Mary the

FISHERMEN'S CHILD.

[*Song. "Turn your glasses upside down"—temperance song and chorus to be written—song with inverted glasses. Picture*]

Mary   group at
    Mother   Percy   back
        Jack   Silas
                                              Hester

END OF PLAY

THE REVEREND GRIFFITH DAVENPORT

CAST OF CHARACTERS

Lafayette Square Theatre, Washington, D.C., January 16, 1899[1]

"Engagement of the Eminent Character Actor
JAMES A. HERNE
and production of his Latest American Play, entitled
REV. GRIFFITH DAVENPORT
(Circuit Preacher)
Founded on Helen H. Gardener's novel "An Unofficial Patriot."

ACT I.

GRIFFITH DAVENPORT		MR. JAMES A. HERNE
BEVERLY DAVENPORT	*his sons*	MR. SYDNEY BOOTH
ROY DAVENPORT		MR. BERT YOUNG
COLONEL ARMOUR, *a lawyer*		MR. NEWTON CHISNELL
HAMILTON BRADLEY		MR. FRANK M. CORNELL
SQUIRE NELSON		MR. LOGAN PAUL
LENGTHY PATTERSON		MR. ROBERT FISCHER
UNCLE NED	*slaves of the Davenports*	MR. LAWRENCE MERTON
PETE		MR. JOSEPH H. HAZLETON
JOHN, *property of Mr. Bradley*		MR. JOHN W. BANKSON
FREE JIM, *a free nigger*		MR. H. G. CARLETON
FREE JIM'S BOY		MASTER KENNETH BARNES
JACK, *a recent purchase of Mr. Nelson*		MR. E. P. SULLIVAN
KATHARINE DAVENPORT		MRS. HERNE
EMMA WEST, *a young Tennessean*		MISS JULIE A. HERNE

[1] This cast is derived from a program of February 13, 1899, at the Herald Square Theatre, New York. Miss Herne assures me, however, that there were no changes.

SUE HARDY, *a young Virginian*	MISS CHRYSTAL HERNE
LITTLE MARGARET, *Davenport's daughter*	GERTRUDE NELSON
SALLIE, *private property of Mrs. Davenport, and married to Mr. Bradley's John*	MISS HELEN ROBERTSON
MAMMY, *Margaret's nurse*	MISS MOLLIE REVEL
AUNT JUDY	MISS SADIE STRINGHAM
TILLY, *the cook*	MISS LUCY NELSON
DINAH	MISS DOROTHY THORNTON
LIPPY JANE	MISS RACHEL BLAKE
THE TWINS, *children of Pete and Tilly*	BY THE TWINS
SALLIE'S BABY	BY HERSELF

ACTS II AND III.

MAJOR HARDY, *father of Sue*	MR. THOMAS M. HUNTER
LEADER OF THE HORSEMEN	MR. H. G. CARLETON

And all of the characters of Act I excepting Free Jim and his son.

ACT IV.

OLIVER P. MORTON, *Governor of Indiana*	MR. WARREN CONLAN

And Griffith Davenport, Roy Davenport, Katharine Davenport, Pete, Uncle Ned, Mammy, Sallie, Aunt Judy, Tilly and little Margaret.

ACT V.

GENERAL LAMOINE, *U.S.A.*	MR. T. C. HAMILTON
SURGEON U.S.A.	MR. FRED JEROME
MAJOR HUNTER, *Chief of Engineer Corps*	MR. PIERRE YOUNG
ORDERLY	MR. ROWLAND EDWARDS
SERGEANT MORRIS	MR. C. C. QUIMBY

Private Bates		MR. THOMAS INCE
Private Hoey		MR. ROBERT GRAY
Private Lang		MR. GEORGE CULVER
Private Stevens		MR. J. HANCOCK HERVEY
Private Alberts		MR. HOWARD RALEIGH
Mr. Monroe	*two old Virginians*	MR. JOHN W. BANKSON
Mr. Sutton		MR. J. B. EARLY
A Confederate's Widow		MISS SUSAN GOOLD
Her Mother		MRS. ISABELLA PRESTON
An Old Southern Woman		MRS. ROSE ATKINS

And Griffith Davenport, Beverly Davenport (now a Confederate captain), Bradley (now a Confederate lieutenant), Major Hardy, Lengthy Patterson, Katharine Davenport and Sue.

ACT I.—VIRGINIA, APRIL 1860.
"COMING EVENTS CAST THEIR SHADOWS"

ACT II.—VIRGINIA, MAY 1860.
THE NOMINATION OF ABRAHAM LINCOLN

ACT III.—VIRGINIA, NOVEMBER 1860.
THE ELECTION OF ABRAHAM LINCOLN

ACT IV.—WASHINGTON, MARCH 1862.
AN UNOFFICIAL PATRIOT

ACT V.—VIRGINIA, APRIL 1864.
FIRST SCENE—THE SHENANDOAH VALLEY. SECOND SCENE—THE NEXT EVENING.

SYNOPSIS OF SCENERY

ACT I. HOUSE AND GROUNDS OF THE DAVENPORTS IN VIRGINIA.

ACT II. AND III. GRIFFITH DAVENPORT'S STUDY AND LIBRARY.

THERE WILL BE AN INTERMISSION OF FOUR MINUTES ONLY BETWEEN ACTS II. AND III.

ACT IV. A ROOM IN THE DAVENPORTS' WASHINGTON HOME. TIME: MARCH 1862.

ACT V. IN THE VALLEY OF THE SHENANDOAH.

THE REVEREND GRIFFITH DAVENPORT

SYNOPSIS OF THE MISSING ACTS

THE scenes of *Griffith Davenport* are laid in Virginia and in Washington, D.C., before and during the Civil War. Griffith Davenport is a Methodist circuit rider, who naturally has learned to know the roads in Virginia. He is a member of an old Virginia family and his communings with God and with nature have deepened the mysticism natural to him. He is opposed to slavery, but he owns a large plantation and a number of slaves, to which are added those that his wife, Katharine, brings him at their marriage. The conflict between them begins at this point for she can see nothing wrong in slavery. In the novel on which the play was based both sons of Griffith Davenport had been Union men, but in the play the eldest son, Beverly, is made a Confederate and Roy, the younger, enters the Union Army. This change adds to the conflict and the drama.

The first act shows the garden of the Davenport estate, with its iron gates, and on one side, the entrance to the fine old mansion. It is a scene of happiness, prosperity and peace. The negro servants, Judy, Pete and others, amble in and out, going about their household tasks in their lazy, easygoing, good-natured fashion, showing the almost ideal conditions under which they live. Most of them have grown up with "Marse and Mis'" and are indulged like a lot of children. They are merry, happy and devoted. Then enters Sally, Katharine's personal maid. She is in a state of helpless misery. She tells the others that the Davenports' neighbor, "Marse Bradley," is forced to sell his coachman, her husband John. If "Marse Grif" won't buy John, it means separation. And Sally and John have a little baby. A hush falls on the other servants as they listen to her. Then they comfort her. *Of course* "Marse Grif" will buy John.

A diversion is caused when the family nurse appears, searching for little Margaret, the Davenports' youngest child, who has run away. She is presently found and returned to her home by Free Jim's boy, the son of an outcast "free nigger," who lives with his father in a wretched cabin on a nearby marsh. When the poor little fellow appears with Margaret, he is almost mobbed by the infuriated Davenport slaves. In their eyes a freed negro, "'thout no fam'ly nor nothin'" is the most despicable of all creatures, fit only for hatred and contempt. They surround the boy, reviling him, until his father, a huge savage in rags enters. With a simple, tragic dignity, he obliges the slaves to fall back, and carries off his boy.

Now another planter, Nelson, comes, and demands to see Griffith. This man is a stern and cruel taskmaster, and his slaves are overworked and rebellious. One of them, Sampson, has tried to run away, and Nelson has handcuffed him to another slave to prevent a second escape. He shows him now to the shocked and horrified Davenport, and tells Griffith that the easygoing ways of his own slaves are corrupting Nelson's establishment. He angrily requests Griffith to keep his "niggers" off the Nelson place. Sampson attempts to justify his action by pleading that he has always been a coachman, and cannot endure the hard labor in the fields which Nelson forces upon him. He begs to be allowed to return to the stables, but Nelson, obdurate, marches him away with an oath.

This scene deeply affects Griffith, and he has hardly recovered from it when Bradley, his neighbor, and John's owner arrives, and pleads with Griffith to buy John, whom he is forced, through gambling debts, to sell, so that husband and wife need not be separated. Katharine too, comes, to add her plea for the almost frantic Sally. But Griffith reminds her of his old resolution, never to buy or sell a human being. Bradley attempts to argue with him. To him, Griffith seems almost a fanatic. Even Katharine is hurt by his seeming hardness. But when Sally herself begs pitifully for her husband, and implores Griffith to buy him for her baby's sake, the man's big heart cannot hold out. He sacrifices his own conviction and buys John. To the others, it seems only that he is making a humanitarian concession. But in his own soul it brings about a climax. Slavery is no longer endurable. He will end it, so far as lies in his power. He will free his own slaves, and if she consents, those of his wife.

He talks it over with Katharine, and she, only half understanding the ethics of the question, but full of faith and love for him, consents. She has long felt that Griffith was not all hers. If it is this question of owning slaves that is dividing them, then, the slaves must be freed.

Act II takes place a few weeks later, in the stately drawing-room, on the evening upon which this momentous decision is to become a fact. Griffith has been to the city, and has returned with the manumission papers. Beverly, his older son, is infuriated at his father's action. He protests to his brother Roy, who sides with his father, and the two boys have their first real disagreement. Beverly feels this division in the family is ominous of larger issues.

"Roy, if this thing ever comes to a war between the North and the South, which side are you going to fight on?"

"On my side," replies Roy, laughing.

Beverly looks at him thoughtfully. "Roy, if I ever met you in a battle, I believe I'd kill you quicker than I would a real Yankee."

Roy takes a deep breath, and then, "I'm sorry, Bev," he says, "but I'm afraid I'll have to give you the chance!"

Presently Griffith assembles his household to hear the momentous announcement. A few curious neighbors are present to witness the strange proceeding. They are all dubious and disapproving, but Griffith is beaming, Katharine reflects his happiness, and Roy is bursting with pride in his father. Only Beverly remains apart. In troop the happy servants, singing and laughing in the anticipation of some sort of treat, for "Marse Grif" always brings them presents when he comes from town. They are counting on tobacco and new calico. And then Griffith Davenport makes them a little speech and shows them some papers. He tells them they are manumission papers, and that now everybody is free. But they do not understand him. They regard him stupidly, wistfully, like a lot of disappointed children. Griffith turns helplessly to his wife, and she tries to explain.

"You're free—you don't belong to us any more," she says.

There is a wail of protest. They, "free niggahs!" They, "not belong to nobody!" They repudiate the idea indignantly. Their pride as members of the family is deeply injured. It is all so different from what Davenport expected. Suddenly Nelson's big Negro, Sampson, bursts into the room, a broken chain dangling from his ankle, a pruning knife in his hand. He has made another attempt to escape. But Nelson, with dogs and men is at his heels. Without even an apology to Mrs. Davenport Nelson rushes in, and orders his men to take Sampson. The men make a lunge, but Sampson holds up his knife. "Ef you come neah me I'll cut mah throat," he said quietly. Griffith, aghast, is impelled to cry, "I'll buy him from you, Nelson!" "I won't sell him!" replies the infuriated Nelson, and makes a move towards Sampson. But the Negro, with a quick movement, plunges the knife into his throat and falls dead before them all. There is a wail of horror from the assembled Negroes. Nelson gives Sampson's body a kick and says, "There goes fifteen hundred dollars!" Then bitterly to Davenport, "This is what your damn anti-slavery theories have come to!" Griffith stands dazed and speechless, and Katharine sinks beside him in a dead faint. Nelson's bitterness towards Davenport gradually communicates itself to the entire countryside, and his old friends and neighbors begin to view Griffith with hatred and alarm. Outwardly, though, all is calm, and life in the Davenport household runs on as before.

Act III shows the Davenport drawing-room on the evening of the Presidential election. The family is gathering for supper when Griffith returns from the polls and announces that he has cast his vote for Abraham Lincoln. Lengthy Patterson, a tall mountaineer, Griffith's devoted follower, appears and asks in his laconic fashion, "Kin I stay here tonight?" They gladly invite him to do so. He stands guard in the drawing-room while the unsuspecting family is at supper. Lengthy has heard that something is in the wind, and presently a mob of angry men storms the house and march into the room. Lengthy bars their way. The family hurries in from the dining-room. Nelson, who is in command, tells Davenport that his voting for Lincoln is the last straw, and commands him to quit the state. Griffith refuses. Someone threatens to burn the house over his head. Katharine says with quiet, bitter dignity, "We will go." A dusty rider hurries in. "Gentlemen," he cries breathlessly, "There is a possibility that Lincoln may be elected!" A groan goes up. The news seems to stun the men. They depart quietly.

Driven from his home, and persecuted for his opinions, something of the martyr's fervor seems now to seize upon Griffith. He gathers his little family about him and prays fervently to God for help and guidance in the new life which they must face, and for the safety of his beloved country in the hour of trial which he foresees must descend upon her.

In the novel Davenport went to Indiana after a brief stay in Washington. For the sake of unity Herne kept the scene of Act IV, here printed, in Washington. In the novel and in the first form of the play Lincoln had sent for Davenport and personally asked him to guide the Union forces through Virginia. This scene, while well written, seemed to be ineffective when the play was in its early rehearsals and then Mrs. Herne, who acted Katharine, saw the difficulty. It was an error in technique to bring to the most important scene a character who overshadowed the hero. Lincoln at once dominated the scene and reduced Griffith Davenport to a secondary position. It was therefore decided to indicate his influence through Governor Morton of Indiana, who as a matter of fact in real life had persuaded the father of the author of the novel to enter the service.

There are two scenes in Act V, in the first of which Griffith Davenport leads the Union troops through his native country until they approach his own home, when he declines to go further. In the play he is captured by the Confederates under his own son, Beverly, and is accused of being a spy. He is, however, searched and his commission being found on him, he becomes a prisoner of war. He is allowed to speak to Katharine before he is taken to prison and the play ends with husband and wife sitting together on the steps of the porch in the moonlight, renewing their vows of love and faith. Katharine asks him to sing an old song of their courtship days, and he begins:

"Oh, if I were king of France—" as the curtain falls.

ACT IV.

"All quiet on the Potomac"

SCENE 1: *Interior of a room in a house in the suburbs of Washington in 1862. The house is on a supposed elevation and through the window—a large square old-fashioned window—in the center may be seen—over the landscape—the White House—and Washington Monument. There is real glass in the window panes—it is a regular March day—rain and sleet beat on the panes at intervals—the room is a sort of study, library and office combined—one or two of the most prominent pieces of furniture were seen in Act III in Virginia—but in the main the furniture is different, colder, more modern—the atmosphere of the place differs from that of the Virginia home.* [NOTE: *the Washington Monument was only partially built in '62.*] *During the entire act there is heard at intervals drum corps, bands, and the noise and movement of marching men—very distant—to suggest war times in Washington in '62. All trimmings are gloss white and ornamented.*

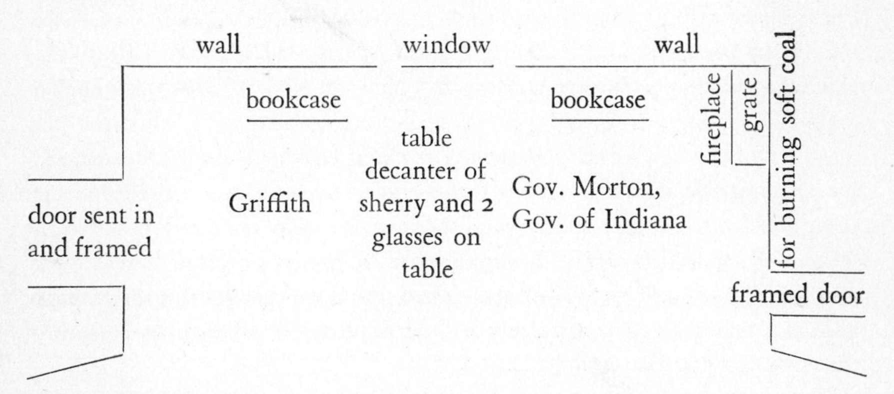

A fine large engraving of Mr. Lincoln—in 1861—in a plain walnut frame must hang so as to be seen by entire audience [NOTE: *Governor Morton must show that the first part of this scene has no interest for him, that he is here upon an important and delicate mission, and that he is puzzled just how to lead up to it successfully, but after he has led up to it he becomes very earnest.*]

Gov. M. [*Abstractedly*] So you've quite settled down here, eh Davenport?

Grif. [*Griffith is smoking and talks and stops and talks to show that he and Morton are intimate and stand upon no ceremony with each other*] Yes —my congregation is poor—my salary small, but I manage to make both ends meet.

Gov. M. [Let's] see, what is your church?

Grif. Calvary—Uncle Ned calls it "De Cavalry." [*Laughs. Morton laughs mechanically. Note: Little Margaret runs on from L. door laughing and jumping on her father's knee—he helps her up—but pays no particular attention to her. Mammy follows her on*]

Mammy. [*In loud whisper*] Heah, heah! [*Laughing*] Yo' paw doan wan fo' to be boddered wif yo' now—yo' come along o' yo' Mammy. [*Carries the child off*]

Gov. M. [*Gets up as child enters, talks through Mammy's scene*] Methodist of course.

Grif. [*Laughs*] Ah! Of course.

Gov. M. [*Walks up and down, stops occasionally—sometimes with his back to audience and talks*] Pity you couldn't have seen your way to taking the position I got for you—Indiana is getting to be a big state—and Professor of Theology at Asbury Institute is a fine position. The College is second to none in the country—and Greencastle is a very pleasant place to live.

Grif. [*Walks*] Yes, I know—but when I found that I couldn't take my black people into the state—not even as hired help, in my own house—I—kind of—[*Winks eye and shakes head*] and then I don't believe Katharine would ever have been satisfied to live so far North.

Gov. M. [*Stops and shows a little more interest*] I never knew a thing about that law in our state—until you brought it to my notice. I don't believe there's a half dozen men in the state who know it now.

Grif. Well, it's there just the same. It's more than a law—it's part of your Constitution. Your Constitution distinctly forbids any person to bring a free nigger into the state of Indiana—that is to live there. I presume it was done to protect labor in your state, I reckon!

Gov. M. I suppose so. Silly though—don't you think so?

Grif. I certainly do. [*Enter Sallie*]

Sal. Mas Grif—Cain Pete an Uncle Naid speak wid yo' fo' a minute?

Grif. Certainly. [*Griffith Davenport, Katharine Davenport, and Roy speak with a Southern accent. Sallie exits leaving the door open—the Parrot of Act I walks in—Judy follows. As Parrot enters, Governor Morton is slightly amused—stops—leans against a table or sits on arm of chair and listens*]

JUDY. [*To Parrot*] Yere—yo' walk yo'se'f outen yere. [*Laughs*] 'Scuse me, Mas Grif—but dis yeah bird—thinks he own dis house, des as ef he was in ol Virginny! [*Catches Parrot*] Come outen yere—What yo' wan' to do—study one o' Mas Grif sahmons? [*Laughs and talks herself off. Pete and Ned have entered in the meantime. Pete is all covered with lime—like a white-washer. Ned is still a general servant*]

GRIF. Well, boys—what is it?

PETE. [*Grinning*] Mas Grif, has yo' got change fo' dis yere shin-plaistah? [*Handing him a fifty-cent note*] Ah done got a job a-whitewashin'—and de lady gimme two dollahs. [*Has fifty-cent notes*] Uncle Naid he say he got ter hab a levee on a fip—an'

GRIF. [*Giving him the change in two notes*] What for?

UNCLE NED. [*Stammers*] 'Twas jes dis way, Mas Grif—Ah was a-comin' home from de market—day fo' yesaday—a—a—an a lady axes me ef Ah cain git her a boy fo' to whitewash—an—an—Ah tole her Ah could—an Ah s—s—sent Pete dar—das dess de whole trufe, Mas Grif.

GRIF. I think Uncle Ned is entitled to his commission, Pete. I'd give him a quarter if I were you. It will encourage him.

PETE. [*Grinning*] Yes sah—all right—Ah des wan'ed to know—dat's all, [*Gives Ned one note*] kase Ah done all de wuk. [*They are going out when Tilly, who has been in the doorway, stops Pete*]

TILLY. [*To Pete*] Heah—yo' gimme dem shin-plaistahs. I'll take car ob dem. [*Pete gives them to her ruefully and they all exit*] They won't buhn no hole in mah pocket!

GOV. M. [*Seating himself in his own chair. Laughing*] Do you have much of that to do?

GRIF. [*Laughing*] Yes, sir! Yes, that's one of my perquisites. [*Laughs*]

GOV. M. You took a pretty big contract when you undertook to free 'em all down there—didn't you?

GRIF. Yes, I freed the slaves—and now I own a lot of free niggers! [*Laughs*]

GOV. M. Why don't you hire 'em out and make 'em earn their own living?

GRIF. [*Cheerily*] The young ones do in a measure—but the old ones own us—we never did own them—they think we'd go to the dogs if they left us—they're just like a lot of children. [*Laughs*]

GOV. M. [*Getting up*] I suppose it'll take 'em some time to adapt themselves to the new condition.

GRIF. A generation or two, I reckon.

GOV. M. [*Going to window*] Reg'lar March day!

GRIF. [*Cheerily*] Yes—He's come in like a sure enough lion this time! [*Laughs*] But that's no reason you should keep walking about the room as if to keep warm. Isn't the room comfortable?

GOV. M. [*Quickly*] Ah yes! Perfectly so—but I'm nervous today—I can't sit still. [*Coming down a little*]

GRIF. Got something on your mind?

GOV. M. Yes. Men in public office in time of war have always something on their minds.

GRIF. Come here and sit down—and enjoy your cigar—and tell me all about it—perhaps I can help you out. [*Lighting his cigar which has gone out*] There are two things in this world I really enjoy—a fine horse and a fine cigar!

GOV. M. Davenport, you can help me. And you are the only man who can. I've got an order to deliver and it is a very delicate one and I don't know just how it is going to be received. It may cost me the friendship of the man I must deliver it to.

GRIF. Why don't you mail it with a fine letter?

GOV. M. [*Getting up and going to window*] That won't do. It is from the President—it is confidential and it is to one of my very dear friends and I am ordered to deliver it in person.

GRIF. From the President? I—I see nothing to do but to deliver it.

GOV. M. [*With his face to the window and his back directly on Griffith*] Did you ever see Mr. Lincoln?

GRIF. Ah yes. I meet him occasionally.

GOV. M. What do you think of him?

GRIF. [*Smiling*] What a question—you know perfectly well what I think of Abraham Lincoln!

GOV. M. [*Turning around*] He's a great man, isn't he?

GRIF. [*Writing*] I thought so when I voted for him—I know so now.

GOV. M. [*Half to himself*] Yes—he's a v-e-r-y g-r-e-a-t man—the South didn't know him or she never would have seceded—doesn't know him yet. [*Coming down*] Did you ever talk with him?

GRIF. [*Astonished*] Gracious—no! He don't know me.

GOV. M. [*Sitting in his chair*] Ah, yes he does! I've told him all about you—he's very much interested in you.

GRIF. That was kind of you and it's good in him—but I can't see what interest the President of the United States can have in a simple citizen like me.

GOV. M. [*Takes his cigar out of his mouth*] He wants to see you. He sent me to fetch you. [*Rises*] Come—I'll introduce you to him.

GRIF. [*Carelessly*] What does he want to see me for?

Gov. M. He wants to offer you a position he has vacant.

Grif. [*Cheerfully*] I don't want any position—I'm not in the political market.

Gov. M. It's not a political position—it's a military one.

Grif. [*Smiling*] I'm not a soldier—I don't know a thing about—

Gov. M. Come along and see Mr. Lincoln—and let him explain himself—he may—

Grif. I'll do that. I shall be very glad to meet Mr. Lincoln—but I don't want any position. [*Rises*] I'm satisfied as I am. [*Enter Roy in uniform of 2nd. Lieut. cavalry*]

Roy. [*Breathlessly*] Where is mother? [*Touches cap to Governor Morton. The Governor returns salute*] Morning, Governor!

Griffith Gov. M.

Roy

Grif. [*Putting table to rights. Without turning points to L.H. door*] Yonder, I reckon. [*To Governor Morton*] Yes, it's—

Roy. Well, father, I've done it!

Grif. Done what? [*Sees him*] Enlisted!

Roy. Yes—19th Indiana—we are to join Grant in the West.

Grif. [*To Governor Morton*] You knew this? [*Governor Morton nods*]

Roy. Are you angry, father?

Grif. No—I'm not angry, my son—but I don't know what your mother will say. [*Calls*] Katharine!

Roy. Don't call her, father, let me tell her. [*Starts towards L. door when it opens and Katharine enters*]

Kath. Did you call me, Griffith? Good morning, Governor—here is a letter from—[*Sees Roy*] Why, Roy—

Roy. [*Trying to be cheery. Throwing his cap on a table*] I have enlisted, Mother.

Kath. Well—I don't know as I am surprised.

Gov. M. [*Enthusiastically*] That is the spirit that's going to save this Union, Mrs. Davenport!

Kath. That spirit is going to make women like me very bitter against the whole thing! To think of my two boys as babies [*Shakes her head*] and to see them now! [*Sighs*]

Roy. [*Tentatively*] I knew Beverly would call me a traitor—but I kind of hoped you would be proud of me.

Kath. [*Wearily*] I suppose I ought to be—proud of you, Roy—everybody else will be—but my boys are worth a good deal more to me—as my boys—

than as heroes. [*Takes a letter from her pocket*] I have a letter from Beverly. Read it. Excuse me, Governor. [*Gives him the letter and exits L. door*]

GRIF. [*To Governor Morton*] Beverly—our oldest boy is in the Confederate Army.

GOV. M. Yes—so you told me—that letter is from him? [*Seating himself*]

GRIF. Yes—read it, Roy.

ROY. Aloud, father?

GRIF. Yes.

ROY. [*Reading*] "Camp Fairfax, March 19, 1862. My own darling Mother: I don't know whether this letter will ever reach you, but I must write it. Jerry is going to try to get through the Yankee lines to post it. I must tell you that you are a grandmother—Jerry brought me the news this morning—we have a beautiful baby girl—the image of her mother, and you know how handsome Sue is. They are all at the old home. Sue sends word that she is very happy—and I'm very happy—happier than I thought I ever could be without you. Do you think that when this war is over, you may come back here and visit us? For I don't suppose you'll ever live South again. I still think father was wrong—but there—that's done. I'm Captain of a Company of Virginia sharp shooters, and we've done some excellent work, and have been personally complimented for bravery and skill—but mother dear, I wish now that the war had never been—not but what I still believe the South right—but I wish this thing could have been settled some other way—but of course it couldn't. I wish slavery had never been—for it cost me my *Mother*. Don't let *Roy* go into the Army, mother. He and I once had some talk about the war, and I said some things to him that I wish now I hadn't said. We are bound to win—for we have the advantage. The Yankees have got to fight us on our own ground all the time—the great decisive battles have got to be fought right here in Virginia—*in the Shenandoah Valley*. They don't know the Valley nor the Mountain passes—we do—we can ambuscade 'em at every turn just as we did at Bull Run—and they know it—that's why it's all quiet on the Potomac, as your newspapers put it—they daren't move—they are afraid of being let into a trap. The fact of their changing Army Commanders isn't going to help 'em. They've made McClellan General in Chief of all their forces —well—they'll never get an able General at the head of their Armies—what they need now are guides. I'm going to have Sue get some pictures taken of her and baby as soon as she's well enough to go out, and I'll try to get one to you. No use to ask you to write because your letters would probably never reach me. Good-bye, mother dear—give my love to father and to Roy—kiss little Madge for me—but keep the dearest and best of me for your own—own

—sweet self—won't you—my—mother. Beverly." [*Griffith is silent. The Governor is very thoughtful*]

GRIF. What *was* the talk you and he had about the war, Roy?

ROY. It was only talk, father—he was angry and so was I.

GOV. M. Come—let us go and see the President!

GRIF. No, I reckon Katharine will want to talk to me now. Excuse me to the President. I'll go with you tomorrow morning.

GOV. M. [*Emphatically*] Tomorrow morning won't do. You've *got* to see him today. [*Seating himself*] Davenport, that boy of yours has hit the nail on the head—our Generals *don't* know that country down there. It's been simply a slaughter of our men every time they've tried to move.

GRIF. Yes, Virginia certainly is a mighty poor country to move an army in, unless a fellow knows it.

GOV. M. *You* know it—every foot of it.

ROY. [*Smiling*] He ought to! He rode it day and night for thirty odd years.

GOV. M. Your knowledge of that country is simply invaluable to Mr. Lincoln just now—and he's got to have it, that's all there is about it. [*Rises and walks about*]

GRIF. [*Excitedly*] Hold on, Governor, hold on! When I first came here we talked that all over and agreed to hoe in our own corn fields.

GOV. M. You can see yourself what the Army is doing down there in Virginia—simply nothing at all! What do you suppose the rebs keep their strongest Generals and their best men right between Washington and Richmond for?

GRIF. Why, that country is the key to the whole situation.

GOV. M. Exactly, and they know that if they can get into Washington they're sure of foreign recognition. [*This sets Griffith to thinking*]

ROY. Gosh! They've come mighty close to Washington more than once.

GOV. M. Close—well, if their Generals had known as much as we did—they'd have walked right up to the Capitol steps. That's what's the matter—they don't know our position and we don't know their country—and there we both are—one's afraid and the other dassn't. If we knew that country—we'd go right into Richmond. You wouldn't like to see our cause lost, would you?

GRIF. I've told you time and again that I believe in the Union. I'm a Union man.

GOV. M. How much of a Union man are you?

GRIF. [*Almost resentfully*] What do you mean by that?

GOV. M. Are you enough of a Union man to help save her?

GRIF. How can I?

Gov. M. [*Drawing his chair in front of table and sitting down again close to Griffith*] I'll tell you something and I know what I'm talking about. If a move isn't made before long—and made right—the Union's gone up in a balloon. [*Pause. Draws chair closer to Griffith's chair, leans forward and whispers aloud*] I'll tell you something more—and this is in strict confidence —[*Slowly and emphatically*] The—President—knows—it—[*Lays his hand on Griffith's knee*] and he hasn't got a soul who knows that country that he dare trust. [*Leans back in his chair and looks steadily at Griffith*] And I've got that from his own lips not half an hour ago. [*Pause*] Now, that's a nice position for the President of the United States to be in—isn't it? [*Changing his whole manner to a determined one*] That's what brought me to Washington. That's what he wants to see you for. *You're* the man he needs—you're the *one* man and the *only* man—who can—

Grif. [*With much feeling, but with great firmness*] No—the South's my home—she's wrong, but I can't fight against her.

Gov. M. Nobody wants you to *fight*. You *voted* for Mr. Lincoln—you helped to put him in the position he is in, and by the Eternal—you've got to sustain him! You've got no right to desert him now when he needs you. It's *treason!*

Grif. No! I'm neutral—I—

Gov. M. [*Vehemently*] There is no neutral ground now. The man who is not *with* Mr. Lincoln now is *against* him.

Grif. [*Smiling*] That's what the fellows in Virginia said to me when I voted for Mr. Lincoln.

Roy. [*Enthused*] Ah! I wish I knew the country as well as father does. I'd—

Gov. M. [*Showing a map which he has carried in his hand. It is wrapped in a black oil cloth*] Here, I want you to run your eye over that and tell me how you would like to move an army by it?

Grif. What is it?

Gov. M. The map of the Shenandoah Valley—and of the mountains and passes of Virginia that General McClellan has been planning this campaign by.

Grif. Where'd you get it?

Gov. M. [*Slowly and impressively*] The President of the United States asked me to show it to *you*. [*The steady gaze of Governor Morton meets the eyes of Griffith, who has stared at him at the words "asked me to show it to you." They look fixedly at each other—Griffith feeling that if he takes that map he will yield, Morton determined he shall take it. After a pause Griffith takes the map and slowly unrolls it. Then Governor Morton changes his tone and becomes colloquial. Indicating place on the map*] There's a strip along there he can't make out. [*Pointing farther along*] That seems to be an opening in the mountains—but—[*Roy has drawn near and is interested in the map*]

GRIF. [*Who has scanned the map carefully, speaks in very positive tones*] No! No! The real opening, the road pass—let me see—what's the scale of miles here? Four—why the road pass is at least five miles farther on! [*He draws an imaginary line with lead pencil which he takes from table*] There! M-m-m—[*Thoughtfully, taking his chin in his hand*] No—n-o-o; this map's all wrong. The road—trends—along here—so. Then you cross the ridge at an angle—so. There ought to be a stream here—oh, pshaw! This map's—where did he get this map? It's no account at all! There are at least seven miles left out right here. Why, right here where they have got those little, insignificant foothills, is one of the most rugged and impassable places in this world! [*Draws several imaginary lines*] Right about here is the Bedolph estate, a splendid place—then as you go up here, you pass into a sort of a pocket. If they got you in there it'd be pretty hard work to get out. But you can cut all that off and go—so—see? There is a mill, and a fine old mill stream, pure water as you ever drank, right here. [*Throws down his pencil*] This map is no good! It would be absolute murder to move an army by that map.

GOV. M. [*Following up his advantage*] The President is aware of that and he is helpless. That's why he turns to you. Now you know why "All is quiet on the Potomac." We daren't move. The Army of the Potomac would mutiny if it knew the real state of affairs.

GRIF. [*Is dazed*] I never saw it in that light before. Just what does he want me to do?

GOV. M. He wants you to be an unofficial patriot.

GRIF. [*Slowly and almost sadly*] An—un—of—ficial—pa—triot—. Ah! [*Shakes his head*]

GOV. M. He's going to send a corps of engineers down there to make a new map of that country. He wants you to lead that corps. You can go in your character of chaplain or—

GRIF. No. If I do this thing, I'll do it outright! I've never seen it as you've made me see it today. If I go I'll ride in the lead, not as a chaplain nor as sutler, but as just what I shall be—God help me—a government guide.

GOV. M. All right. Now about your pay. How does a colonel's commission and pay strike you? [*He says this as if it were an extraordinary offer, one which no sane man would refuse*]

GRIF. [*Indignantly*] Commission? Pay? Am I to understand that he offers to pay me to—

Gov. M. [*Quickly and pacifically*] No! No! But you have got to be carried on the pay roll. You've got to have *grub-rations*. The commission is for your personal security. It is necessary, in case of—of—accident, it secures you the right of honorable exchange and fair treatment as a—a—prisoner of war.

Grif. I shall be a spy, all the same, in my own heart—I shall be a spy. I can't do it. I can *not* do it!

Gov. M. Faugh! I've no patience with you. Did you ever see a panic of wounded men after a battle?

Grif. [*Horrified*] Oh! My God—yes! I saw McDowell's army cross Long Bridge yonder [*Points*] on the 21st day of last July—young men and boys—[*Unconsciously embraces Roy*] singing, cheering, filled with the ecstasy of life and youth and joy. And I saw their retreat from Bull Run the next day. My God! I've seen nothing else since, day or night!

Gov. M. [*Sternly*] You could have prevented that disaster, and you will have yourself to blame if the President of the United States and the Generals of the Union Army have to account for another *like* it. And now I'm going to see the President. Will you come?

Grif. No. Not today. [*Rolls up the map and offers it to the Governor*]

Gov. M. [*Refuses to take it*] No, I want you to think it over, and I want you to read this. [*Takes official document, which is in an official envelope, from his breast pocket and hands it to Griffith, who takes it in a nerveless sort of way, as if he had no power to resist*]

Grif. What's this?

Gov. M. The order I was commanded by the President to deliver in person to a very dear friend. [*To Roy, while Griffith reads the paper*] I expect to hear good reports of you. [*Then goes down to Griffith; slowly*] That's a p-e-r-e-mptory order. [*Takes out watch*] I shall expect you to meet me at Willards at four o'clock. It is 3:15 now, and we will go over there together. [*Griffith is in a daze. The Governor starts to go, stops, comes back*] And by the way, you might as well make up your mind not to come back to the house for the present. You'll probably have to go into commission at once. Four o'clock, at Willards. Good-bye. [*To Roy, who shows him to the door*] Good-bye, my son. [*Shakes hands with Roy. Roy touches his forehead in military salute. The words of the Governor have inspired him with pride. Closes the door just in time to see his father, who has read the paper, fall into a chair with his head buried in his arms. The paper falls on the floor*]

Roy. What is it, father? [*Sees the paper, picks it up. Enthusiastically, with a smile, reads:*]

Executive Mansion,
March 16, 1862
Oliver P. Morton, Governor of Indiana:
Order your man, Davenport, to report to me immediately.
(Seal) *A. Lincoln*

[*Pause*] You've got to obey *that* order, father.

GRIF. I can't, Roy. I can't!

ROY. [*Partly astonished and partly disappointed that his father does not respond to the order*] You must—you can't help yourself.

GRIF. What will your mother say? [*His head still buried in his arms*]

ROY. [*Decisively*] I don't know, but you have got to obey that order. [*Ends in fatalistic half whisper. Enter Katharine L. door. She is dressed for walking. She is intent on buttoning her gloves, and does not look up as she speaks*]

KATH. Griffith, I'm going out for a walk. Is there—

ROY. [*Cheerily*] Do you want me to go with you, mother?

KATH. No—I—[*Looks up, sees Griffith bowed down. Springs to him*] Why, Griffith! What's the matter? Has anything happened? [*Griffith merely shakes his head and swings his body*]

KATH. [*With more emphasis*] What's the matter? Can't you speak? Roy —what—[*Turns her head, sees the paper which Roy is turning over in his hands. She stops, turns pale and sick. Whispers*] Beverly—[*She can scarcely speak*] When—how—where—

ROY. [*Extending the paper. Shakes his head to indicate "No"*] Mother, the President orders father to report to him immediately.

KATH. [*With a long breath*] Oh! Mercy! Why didn't you say so? You gave me a dreadful shock. I thought Beverly had been killed. [*Takes the paper, tries to command herself. Reads*] Why—this is to Governor Morton. Oh! I see! "Order your man, Davenport, to report to me immediately, A. Lincoln." [*Indignantly*] Well—I—your *man,* Davenport—the presumption! [*To Griffith*] What are you going to do with this, Griffith? [*Holding the telegram towards him*]

GRIF. [*Hesitatingly*] I don't know—yet—

KATH. [*Surprised*] Don't *know?*

GRIF. I was trying to think what I ought to do—what would you do, if you were me?

KATH. I'd tear it to tatters! [*Attempting to suit the action to the word*]

ROY. Mother, don't—

KATH. [*Almost shrieks*] Let me alone! [*Then to Griffith in a quieter but still intense tone*] That's what I'd do with it.

GRIF. [*Rising and quietly taking the paper from her*] I wouldn't tear it, Katharine, if I were you. That won't help matters.

KATH. What does this—*man,* Lincoln, want with you, Griffith?

GRIF. [*Slowly*] I reckon he wants me to give him a key to the Shenandoah Valley.

KATH. A—key—to—the—Shenan—

GRIF. McClellan has 100,000 men down there in the Army of the Potomac, and he can't move 'em—without—

KATH. You don't mean to say—that he wants you to guide his Army?

GRIF. I reckon that's about what it amounts to. He wants me to map the Shenandoah Valley and mountain passes for him.

KATH. [*Indignant*] Oh, Griffith—what an insult!

ROY. [*Astonished*] Insult? Why, mother! It's an honor.

KATH. [*Indignantly*] Is it—well—I'd rather a man would horsewhip me—than to offer me such an honor!

ROY. Governor Morton says it's father's duty.

KATH. Governor Morton is not dictator in this family. [*Getting more and more excited as she goes on; tears off her right glove*] I'll answer this!

GRIF. Wait a minute—let us go slow—let us talk the thing over. Now as I look at it—this—[*Holding up the paper*] is a peremptory military order.

KATH. [*Still indignant*] But you are not one of this man's soldiers.

GRIF. [*Continuing*] And it is signed by the President of the United States.

KATH. [*Amazed*] Why, Griffith! You surely have no idea of obeying that order?

GRIF. I don't know that I've got the right to refuse.

KATH. [*Astounded*] Griffith!

GRIF. This is an extraordinary case. Here is a man at the head of a great nation—

KATH. [*Proudly*] The *North is not* the nation. I'm a Southern woman. Virginia is my home. The people there are my people. I did not leave it because I didn't love it, or because I was not happy there; I left it because *you* were not happy there. [*Begins to unconsciously, half angrily, excitedly, take off hat, shawl and coat, throwing them on chair or table as she gets them off*]

GRIF. Katharine—

KATH. I left refinement, all my old and congenial friends—and everything I had been accustomed to all my life. I have never pretended that it wasn't a sacrifice on my part—I am not a hypocrite—I realize the difference between my home and this house—I never will, never *can* love this place. [*Contemptuously*] These narrow, penurious, unsympathetic Northern people are as far from me as day is from night. I don't hate them, but I've nothing in common with them. But I do love *you* and I've been happy, *even here—with you*. I'll follow you into the frigid zone, if you ask me to—but when the President of the Yankee States orders you to leave me and guide his Army against *my country* and *my people,* I say *"No"!* You shall not do it.

GRIF. There are *times*—when patriotism—

KATH. Griffith, this is a *brutal* war. You have said so yourself a hundred times. It isn't a war against oppression; it hasn't the righteousness of *1776* to sanctify it. It's a *factional fight*—it's a *political war!* Patriotism! Think of our two brave boys with guns in their hands, ready to murder each other in the name of patriotism, and now you want to kill me [*Weeps*] under the same delusion.

GRIF. Katharine! This is the first time you and I have come to words on this question. I didn't believe we ever could have done so. I thought we understood each other too well for that. You are very bitter against the North. I can't blame you for that, but I—

KATH. [*Earnestly*] No, Griffith—it's not that—I pledge you my word, it's not that—it's *you,* my *husband*. I'm frightened—I've lost my two boys—I expected that—I was sort of prepared for that—but oh!—*you,* Griffith—I never expected to lose *you*. I've always sort of hoped that when the time came I might go first. I don't want you in this war on either side. Oh, Griffith—my husband, don't go—for God's sake, don't go—don't leave me here alone!

GRIF. Katharine, [*Pointing to picture*] that is Abraham Lincoln, the President of the United States, after his inauguration March 4, 1861. [*Taking cabinet photo of Lincoln from top of bookcase*] This is Abraham Lincoln March 1, 1862. Do you see the change in the face? No human being has ever suffered in a life time what this man has suffered in one short year. Men think it is a great thing to be the president of a great nation; and so it is, in time of peace; but ah, Katharine, in time of war! President Lincoln hasn't got a man he dare trust to map this country. [*Shows map*] Look at that. [*Getting excited*] He turns to me, and he says, "Davenport, I need *you*. I answered when you all needed me. Now, when I need you—" He points his accusing finger at me and says, "There is but one way to shorten this war, to lessen the awful slaughter, the carnage and suffering, on *both* sides. There is but one man who knows how to do this, and that man is" [*Pointing to himself*] *"you*. And you have not done your duty to your country. No sir, nor to your God, until you have done that." [*Falls into a chair overcome with his emotions, and buries his face in his arms*]

KATH. [*Almost heart-broken*] I know—I know—but ah—to think of you, my husband, guiding an army against—

GRIF. Look at that bridge. Do you remember that bridge on the 22d of last July? [*Points out of window in direction of Long Bridge*] Do you see young sons like yours dragging bleeding limbs across it? Do you see terror stricken horses trampling down those wounded boys?

KATH. [*Horrified*] Don't, Griffith! For God's sake, don't!

GRIF. It is for God's sake. I pray to my God that I may never see another such day in my life. If I knew how to prevent a railroad accident—what would you think of me if I did not prevent it?

KATH. You have sacrificed so much already, Griffith. You have impoverished yourself—

GRIF. I know, I know—

KATH. The people down there loved you so before. I hoped that after all perhaps we might some day go back there again, but now—[*Shakes her head*] every man, woman and child in Virginia will hate—and despise you—

GRIF. The people down there never understood me. But *you*—you do. Would you ever have loved me—had I been different?

KATH. [*Going to him. Firmly*] No.

GRIF. Will you respect me now, if I do not respect myself?

KATH. No.

GRIF. Then kiss me, and tell me to go.

KATH. Do you realize what you ask of me?

GRIF. Yes.

KATH. Is there no other way?

GRIF. I see none.

KATH. Ah, Griffith! How can I say it? Suppose anything should happen to you? That you should be taken? [*Breaking down*] I'd never forgive myself. I believe I'd kill myself. [*Recovering herself*] Griffith, I have made sacrifice after sacrifice for you. Now you come to me and ask me to make the supreme sacrifice of my life. I rebel. I cannot do it. [*Decisively*] I *will* not do it. [*Changing her tone*] Ah, Griffith, my husband, you are all I have! I love you —I tell you I love you. I cannot give you up!

GRIF. Katharine, this is not a question of your life or my life, or of our love for each other. The life of the nation is at stake. Abraham Lincoln calls out to me, "Help me to save the nation. Help me to save this nation." I can't shut my ears to his pitiful cry.

KATH. You solemnly believe it your duty to go, do you?

GRIF. Yes, Katharine. It is a duty I owe my fellow men on both sides of Mason and Dixon's line. It is a duty I owe to the man I helped to make responsible for this war. It is a duty I owe the government under which I live, and of which I am an infinitesimal part.

KATH. [*Seeing that argument is useless*] Well, then—go! [*This last with a supreme effort*]

GRIF. [*Relieved*] I knew I could depend on you. You are the bravest little woman in the world.

ROY. [*Going to her tenderly*] God bless you, my mother.

KATH. [*Smiling sadly*] Why! I'm quite a hero! Go, Griffith, but before you go, I want to tell you one thing. I will go too.

GRIF. [*Astonished*] Go—where?

KATH. Home. To my home. To Virginia.

GRIF. [*Horror-stricken*] Katharine—you will not do—

KATH. I will do just what you are going to do. Help the cause I believe in.

GRIF. You will not do this?

KATH. Why not? If the Army of the Potomac needs you, the Army of Virginia needs me.

GRIF. To think of you on a battle field or in a hospital—

KATH. Where can I be more useful now than among our sick and suffering soldiers?

GRIF. If I promise you—

KATH. Promises will not hold us together now. We have come to the fork in the road.

GRIF. I'm not going to fight, Katharine. [*Smiling*]

KATH. I believe I'd rather you were. I believe I'd rather see you with a sword or a gun in your hand than to see you guiding an Army against my country, against my people, against my son—

GRIF. [*Pleading*] Tell me that I shall find you here when I return.

KATH. No! When you return I'll come back, if you want me, but I must go now. I must do my duty as I see it—just as you do yours.

GRIF. You are right. Your heart is there. It is your duty to go.

KATH. When are you to see your president?

GRIF. [*As if talking from a dream or reverie. Looks at watch*] Now. I must go *now*.

KATH. Tell him he must send me and my household through the lines. I shall take Sallie and Judy, Mammy and Uncle Ned; the others must shift for themselves. [*Griffith's lips part as if to protest. She divines his thought*] I *forbid* you to accept any position under him, unless he agrees to do this for me. It is my right.

GRIF. He shall do this for you or do without me. Good-bye.

KATH. Good-bye, Griffith.

GRIF. Won't you kiss me?

KATH. Yes. [*Does so tenderly and lovingly*]

GRIF. Sometimes we come to a fork in a road, Katharine—and both branches meet again a few miles further on. Good-bye. [*Katharine totters after him to the door as if to recall him; then goes to table and leans against it in a heartbroken way, and is immersed in the thought of her loneliness and of how she is to get away from this place quickly. Griffith goes to Roy, takes him in his arms. They kiss each other on the cheek. Griffith pantomimes to Roy to comfort his mother. Roy signifies yes. Griffith goes slowly and silently out at street door, looking at watch as he goes*]

ROY. [*Going to her*] Mother! [*Softly, putting arms around her. Sallie enters. She is crying softly*]

SAL. Mis Kate, John wan's ter shake han's. He reg'men oddahed to de fron'.

KATH. Oh! Yes—John's a soldier too.

SAL. 'Es, Mis Kate. Kinder sojah—not reg'lah. He—

ROY. [*Enthusiastically*] Aren't you proud of him, Sallie?

SAL. I was proud at fust, Mas Roy, but seems des as ef Ah coulden be proud terday. [*Sees Roy's uniform for the first time*] Oh, Mas Roy—is yo'— [*Sort of horrified*]

KATH. When do you go, Roy?

ROY. Tomorrow, mother.

KATH. Sallie, we must get ready to leave this place. [*Picking up hat and walking things. Band, distant march*]

SAL. [*Stops crying, loses all interest in herself and her own trouble, frightened and anxious*] Leave heah, Mis Kate? Wha' fo'? Whar we all gwan ter *now*?

KATH. [*Tottering towards the door opposite from that which Davenport made his exit, speaks slowly, brokenly*] Back to Virginia. [*Goes slowly off L.2.E.*]

SAL. Oh! Mas' Roy, wha's happen—wha—

ROY. Hush! She's going back to Beverly, that's all. [*Motions her to follow her mistress. Sallie goes slowly out at door L.2.E., looking back at Roy, mystified and scared. Band music (march) nearer. Roy puts on his cap and goes to the window. March louder*]

CURTAIN

BIBLIOGRAPHY

JAMES A. HERNE

SHORE ACRES AND OTHER PLAYS. Revised by Mrs. James A. Herne. Biographical Note by Julie A. Herne, 1928. Contains *Shore Acres, Sag Harbor, Hearts of Oak*.

MARGARET FLEMING. In *Representative American Plays,* 1930 and later editions, edited by Arthur Hobson Quinn.

BIOGRAPHICAL AND CRITICAL

Herne, James A. "Old Stock Days in the Theatre," *Arena,* Vol. VI (Sept. 1892), pp. 401-16.

Herne, James A. "Art for Truth's Sake in the Drama," *Arena,* Vol. XVII (Feb. 1897), pp. 361-70.

Corbin, John. "Drama," *Harper's Weekly,* Vol. XLIII (Feb. 11 and March 4, 1899), pp. 139 and 213. [Griffith Davenport]

Flower, B. O. "Mask or Mirror," *Arena,* Vol. VIII (Aug. 1893), pp. 304-13.

Garland, Hamlin. "Mr. and Mrs. Herne," *Arena,* Vol. IV (Oct. 1891), pp. 543-60.

Garland, Hamlin. "On the Road with James A. Herne," *Century Magazine,* Vol. LXXXVIII, N.S. (Aug. 1914), pp. 574-81.

"An Appreciation: James A. Herne, Actor, Dramatist and Man," Articles by Hamlin Garland, J. J. Enneking and B. O. Flower. *Arena,* Vol. XXVI (Sept. 1901), pp. 282-91.

Hapgood, Norman. *The Stage in America,* pp. 61-9.

Howells, W. D. "Editor's Study," *Harper's Magazine,* Vol. LXXXIII (Aug. 1891), pp. 478-9. [Margaret Fleming]

Quinn, Arthur Hobson. *A History of the American Drama from the Civil War to the Present Day,* Vol. I, Chap. vi, "James A. Herne and the Realism of Character," pp. 125-62. Revised edition in one volume, 1936.

Tiempo, Marco. "James A. Herne in Griffith Davenport," *Arena,* Vol. XXII (Sept. 1899), pp. 375-82.

America's Lost Plays

VOLUME I

DION BOUCICAULT

Plays: *Forbidden Fruit, Dot, Flying Scud, Louis XI, Robert Emmet, Presumptive Evidence (Mercy Dodd)*

EDITED BY ALLARDYCE NICOLL AND F. THEODORE CLOAK

VOLUME II

WILLIAM DUNLAP

Plays: *Thirty Years; or, The Gambler's Fate, False Shame; or, The American Orphan in Germany*

EDITED BY ORAL S. COAD

VOLUME III

GEORGE HENRY BOKER

Plays: *The World a Mask, Glaucus, The Bankrupt*

EDITED BY SCULLEY BRADLEY

VOLUME IV

MISCELLANEOUS

Plays: *Across the Continent,* by J. J. McCloskey, *Rosedale,* by Lester Wallack, *Davy Crockett,* by Frank Murdoch, *Sam'l of Posen,* by G. H. Jessop, *Our Boarding House,* by Leonard Grover

EDITED BY THE LATE ISAAC GOLDBERG, COMPLETED BY HUBERT HEFFNER

VOLUMES V AND VI

JOHN HOWARD PAYNE

Plays: *Trial without Jury: or, The Magpie and the Maid, Mount Savage, The Boarding Schools, The Two Sons-in-Law, Mazeppa, The Spanish Husband, The Last Duel in Spain, Woman's Revenge, The Italian Bride, Romulus, The Black Man*

EDITED BY CODMAN HISLOP AND W. R. RICHARDSON

VOLUME VII

JAMES A. HERNE

Plays: *Drifting Apart, The Minute Men, Within an Inch of His Life, Griffith Davenport (fragment)*

EDITED BY ARTHUR HOBSON QUINN

VOLUME VIII

RECENT MELODRAMAS

Plays: *A Royal Slave,* by Clarence Bennett, *The Great Diamond Robbery,* by Edward W. Alfriend and A. C. Wheeler, *From Rags to Riches,* by Charles A. Taylor, *No Mother to Guide Her,* by Lillian Mortimer, *Billy the Kid,* by Walter Woods

EDITED BY GARRETT H. LEVERTON

VOLUME IX

CHARLES HOYT

Plays: *A Bunch of Keys, A Midnight Bell, A Milk White Flag, A Trip to Chinatown, A Temperance Town*

EDITED BY DOUGLAS L. HUNT

VOLUME X

BRONSON HOWARD

Plays: *Knave and Queen (Ivers Dean), Old Love Letters, Hurricanes, Baron Rudolph, The Banker's Daughter, One of Our Girls*

EDITED BY ALLAN G. HALLINE

VOLUME XI

STEELE MACKAYE

Plays: *Rose Michel, Won at Last, In Spite of All, An Arrant Knave*

EDITED BY PERCY MACKAYE

VOLUME XII

ROBERT MONTGOMERY BIRD

Plays: *The Cowled Lover, Caridorf, News of the Night, 'Twas All for the Best*

EDITED BY EDWARD H. O'NEILL

VOLUME XIII

RICHARD PENN SMITH

Plays: *The Sentinels, The Bombardment of Algiers, William Penn (fragment), Shakespeare in Love, A Wife at a Venture, The Last Man*

EDITED BY H. W. SCHOENBERGER AND RALPH H. WARE

VOLUME XIV

MISCELLANEOUS

Plays: *Metamora,* by J. A. Stone, *Tancred,* by J. A. Stone (one act), *Signor Marc,* by J. H. Wilkins, *The Battle of Stillwater,* by H. J. Conway, *The Crock of Gold,* by Silas S. Steele, *Job and His Children,* by Joseph M. Field, *The Duke's Motto,* by John Brougham, *The Spy,* by Charles P. Clinch, *The Usurper,* by J. S. Jones

EDITED BY EUGENE R. PAGE

VOLUME XV

ROYALL TYLER

Plays: *The Island of Barrataria, The Origin of the Feast of Purim, Joseph and His Brethren, The Judgment of Solomon*

EDITED BY ARTHUR WALLACE PEACH AND GEORGE FLOYD NEWBROUGH

VOLUME XVI

HISTORICAL AND ROMANTIC PLAYS

Plays: *Monte Cristo (as played by James O'Neill), Hippolytus,* by Julia Ward Howe, *Mistress Nell,* by George Hazleton, *Becky Sharp,* by Langdon Mitchell, *The Warrens of Virginia,* by William C. deMille

EDITED BY J. B. RUSSAK

VOLUME XVII

HENRY C. DeMILLE

IN COLLABORATION WITH DAVID BELASCO AND CHARLES BARNARD

Plays: *The Main Line, The Wife, Lord Chumley, The Charity Ball, Men and Women*

EDITED BY ROBERT HAMILTON BALL

VOLUME XVIII

DAVID BELASCO

Plays: *La Belle Russe, The Stranglers of Paris, The Heart of Maryland, The Girl I Left Behind Me, Naughty Anthony*

EDITED BY GLENN HUGHES AND GEORGE SAVAGE

VOLUME XIX

BARTLEY CAMPBELL

Plays: *The White Slave, My Partner, The Galley Slave, Peril, Fairfax, The Virginian*

EDITED BY NAPIER WILT

VOLUME XX

AUGUSTIN DALY

Plays: *Man and Wife, Divorce, The Big Bonanza, Pique, Needles and Pins*

EDITED BY CATHERINE STURTEVANT